We thank the following organizations for their endorsement of this International Conference:

• Alliance for Democracy • Alliance for Global Justice • Baltimore Nonviolence Center • Bayan USA • Black Alliance for Peace • Canadian Peace Congress • CODEPINK • Comitato No Guerra No Nato - Italy • Coop Anti-War Cafe / #Aufstehen Berlin-Mitte, Germany • Denver Peace Council • Global Network Against Weapons and Nuclear Power in Space • Greater New Haven Peace Council • Hands Off Syria Coalition • International Action Center • Iraq Solidarity, Sweden • Mobilization Against War and Occupation (MAWO) — Canada • New York Solidarity with Vieques • No Dal Molin • Nuclear Age Peace Foundation • Okinawa Peace Action Center • PCUSA • Peace in Our Times • Peoples Movement — Gluaiseacht an Phobail • Popular Resistance • Queens Peace Council, NY • Sacred Ground Historical Reclamation Project • Syria Solidarity Movement • Task Force on the Americas • United National Antiwar Coalition (UNAC) • U.S. Peace Council • Virginia Defenders for Freedom, Justice & Equality • Veterans For Peace • Women's International League for Peace and Freedom U.S. Section • World Beyond War • World Peace Council

*Proceedings of the First International Conference
Against US/NATO Military Bases*
November 16-18, 2018
Liberty Hall, Dublin, Ireland

ISBN: 978-0-578-52880-9

International Conference Against US/NATO Military Bases

Liberty Hall — Dublin, Ireland
November 16-18, 2018

Organized by:

Peace And Neutrality Alliance (Ireland)
Coalition Against U.S. Foreign Military Bases (USA)

This was the first International Conference Against US/NATO Military Bases organized by the Global Campaign Against US/NATO Military Bases. This conference was the product of months of discussion and planning by representatives of more than thirty peace, justice and environmental organizations from around the world. The goal of Global Campaign is to create a broad-based coalition of peace, justice and environmental organizations and activists throughout the world for an ongoing movement to close all US/NATO military bases in all countries. Please sign our Unity Statement and ask your organization, your friends and your colleagues to do the same. Thank you.

Peace and Neutrality Alliance (PANA) — Ireland • Coalition Against U.S. Foreign Military Bases — USA • World Peace Council (WPC) • Movimiento Cubano por la Paz y la Soberania de los Pueblos (MOVPAZ) — (Cuba) • Centro Brasileiro de Solidariedade aos Povos e Luta pela Paz (CEBRAPAZ) — (Brazil) • Stop the War Coalition — (UK) • Okinawa Peace Action Center — (Japan) • Japan Peace Committee — (Japan) • Gangjeong International Team — (Jeju, Korea) • Conselho Português para a Paz e Cooperação — (Portugal) • German Peace Council — (Germany) • Belgrade Forum for a World of Equals — (Serbia) • Peace Committee of Turkey — (Turkey) • Cyprus Peace Council — (Cyprus) • Greek Committee for International Detente and Peace (EEDYE) — (Greece) • Philippine Peace & Solidarity Council (PPSC) — (Philippines) • Foro Contra la Guerra Imperialista y la OTAN — (Spain) • Palestinian Committee for Peace and Solidarity —

(Palestine) • Canadian Peace Congress — (Canada) • Lebanese Peace Council — (Lebanon) • Peace and Solidarity Committee in Israel — (Israel) • Czech Peace Movement — (Czech Republic) • South African Peace Initiative — (South Africa) • All India Peace and Solidarity Organization — (India) • Nepal Peace & Solidarity Council — (Nepal) • Swiss Peace Movement — (Switzerland) • British Peace Assembly — (Britain) • International Action for Liberation (INTAL) — (Belgium) • International League of Peoples Struggle — (Netherlands) • Comitato Contro La Guerra Milano (CCLGM) — (Italy) • Jamaica Peace Council — (Jamaica) • Campaign for Nuclear Disarmament — (UK) • Independent and Peaceful Australia Network — (Australia) • Escuela de Paz Colombia — (Colombia) • Guyana Peace Council — (Guyana) • Comitato No Guerra No Nato — (Italy) • Task Force on the Americas — USA • Dissent: Voices of Conscience — USA • The Pacific Institute of Resource Management — New Zealand • Shannonwatch — Ireland • Campaign Stopp Air Base Ramstein

Global Campaign Against US/NATO Military Bases
Unity Statement

We, the undersigned peace, justice and environmental organizations and individuals from around the world, endorse the following Statement of Unity and commit ourselves to working together in a broad-based international campaign to organize an International Conference Against all US/NATO Military Bases, with the goal of raising public awareness and organizing non-violent mass resistance throughout the world against all US, NATO and EU military bases, and their military missions around the world.

While we may have our differences on other issues, we all agree that US/NATO military bases are the principal instruments of imperial global domination and primary causes of devastating environmental and health impacts through wars of aggression and occupation, and that the closure of the US/NATO military bases is one of the first necessary steps toward a just, peaceful and sustainable world. Our belief in the urgency of this necessary step is based on the following facts:

While we are opposed to all foreign military bases, we do recognize that the United States maintains the highest number of military bases outside its territory, estimated at almost 1,000 (95% of all foreign military bases in the world). Presently, there are US military bases in every Persian Gulf country except Iran.

In addition, the United States alone has 19 naval air carriers (and 15 more planned), each as part of a Carrier Strike Group, composed of roughly 7,500 personnel, and a carrier air wing of 65 to 70 aircraft — each of which can be considered a floating military base.

These bases are centers of aggressive military actions, threats of political and economic expansion, sabotage and espionage, and crimes against local populations. In addition, these military bases are the largest users of fossil fuel in the world, heavily contributing to environmental degradation.

The annual cost of these bases to US taxpayers alone is approximately $156 billion. The cost of these military bases drains funds that can be used to fund human needs and enable our countries to provide necessary services for the people.

NATO, as the armed wing of the United Sates and the European Union, is expanding further to the east to safeguard its control of energy resources and pipelines, spheres of influence and markets for the sake of big capital and transnational corporations. The European Union, in particular, is advancing alone or/and with NATO to its further militarization with the Permanent Structural Cooperation (PESCO) and its powerful EU army.

All governments of the member states of NATO bear direct individual responsibility for NATO's aggressive policies, and the increase of their military budgets to 2% of GDP while their people are suffering under severe austerity measures and the economic crisis caused by their militaristic policies.

All of this has pushed the world toward ever-increasing militarization, and to ever-deepening antagonism between the US and its NATO allies, on the one hand, and the rest of the world, on the other. Stationed throughout the world, almost 1,000 in number, US/NATO military bases are symbols of the ability of the United States to intrude into the lives of sovereign nations and peoples.

Many individual national movements — for example, in Okinawa, Italy, Jeju Island Korea, Diego Garcia, Cyprus, Greece, Serbia, Spain, Ghana, Czech Republic and Germany — are demanding closure of the US/NATO bases on their territory. The base that the U.S. has illegally occupied the longest, for over a century, is Guantánamo Bay, whose existence constitutes a violation of International Law and the Cuban people's right to sovereignty. Since 1959 the government and people of Cuba have demanded that the government of the United States return the Guantánamo territory to Cuba.

The NATO states' military bases in other countries are NOT in defence of their national, or global security. They are the military expression of imperialist intrusion into the lives of sovereign countries on behalf of the dominant financial, political, and military interests of the ruling elite. Whether invited in or not by domestic interests that have agreed to be junior partners, no country, no peoples, no government, can claim to be able to make decisions totally in the interest of their people, with foreign troops on their soil representing interests antagonistic to those of their peoples.

We express our solidarity with the just causes of the peoples in their struggle against foreign military aggression, occupation and interference in their internal affairs, and their devastating environmental and health impacts, and for a world of real peace and social and environmental justice.

We must all unite to actively oppose the existence of all US/NATO military bases on foreign soil and call for their immediate closure. We invite all forces of peace, social and environmental justice to join us in our renewed global effort to achieve this shared goal.

Proceedings of the First International Conference Against US/NATO Military Bases

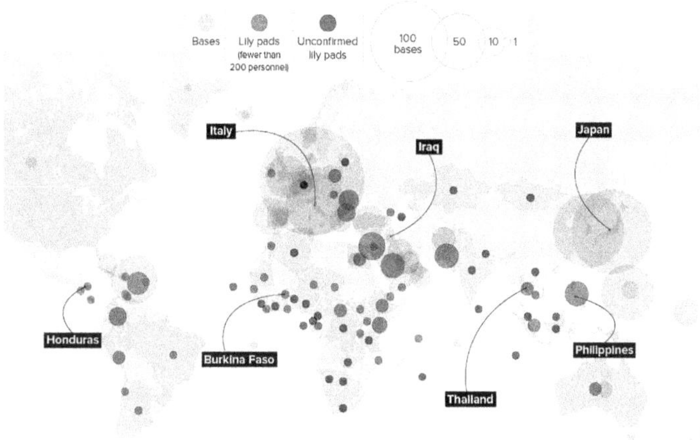

Liberty Hall
Dublin, Ireland
November 16-18, 2018

Table of Contents

Conference Schedule

Friday, November 16:

3:00 – 5:00 PM — Rally at Dublin GPO Against US/NATO Military Bases

---

5:00 – 7:00 PM — Dinner

7:00 – 10:00 PM — Public Meeting: International Night
Chair: Dr. Edward Horgan
PANA, World BEYOND War, Ireland

Welcoming Remarks:

— **Roger Cole,** Chair, Peace And Neutrality Alliance (PANA), Ireland
— **Dr. Bahman Azad**, Coordinator, Coalition Against U.S. Foreign Military Bases (CAUSFMB), USA

Keynote Speakers:

— **Aengus Ó Snodaigh, TD**, Dail Eireann [Irish Parliament], Ireland
— **Clare Daly, TD**, Dail Eireann, Ireland

International Night Speakers:

— **Mairead Maguire**, Nobel Peace Laureate, Ireland
— **Socorro Gomes**, President, World Peace Council (WPC)
— **Alfred L. Marder**, President, U.S. Peace Council, USA
— **Solvio Platero**, President, MOVPAZ, Cuba
— **Dr. John Lannon**, Member of the National Executive, PANA; Shannonwatch, Ireland

— **Hiroji Yamashiro**, Director, Okinawa Peace Action Center, Japan
— **Moara Crivelente**, Executive Director, CEBRAPAZ, Brazil
— **Dr. Stelios Sofocli**, President, Cyprus Peace Council, Cyprus
— **Fulvio Grimaldi**, Professional journalist and war correspondent, Italy
— **Lucsa Wirl**, Stop Air Base Ramstein, Germany
— **Grigoris Anagnostou**, Organizing Secretary of the Greek Committee for International Detente and Peace (EEDYE), Greece

Musical Performance

Saturday, November 17:

8:00 - 9:00 AM — Registration and Check-in

9:00 – 9:45 AM — Opening Session: Keynote

Chair: Ajamu Baraka
Black Alliance for Peace, USA

Keynote Speaker:

— **Dr. Aleida Guevara**, Cuba

**10:00 – 11:15 AM — Plenary 1:
Militarism, Nuclear Weapons, and Military Bases**

Chair: Dr. Margaret Flowers
Popular Resistance, USA

Speakers:

— **Iraklis Tsavdaridis**, Executive Secretary, World Peace Council, Greece
— **Dr. Dave Webb**, Chair, Campaign for Nuclear Disarmament (CND), UK
— **Joe Lombardo**, Co-Coordinator, United National Antiwar Coalition, USA

11:30 – 12:45 PM: Plenary 2:
Environmental and Health Impact of Military Bases
Chair: Senator Grace O'Sullivan
Green Party, Ireland

Speakers:

— **Dr. Zuhal Okuyan**, Chairwoman, Peace Committee of Turkey
— **Milan Krajca**, Chairman, Czech Peace Movement, Czech Republic
— **Pat Elder**, Civilian Exposure, World BEYOND War, USA

12:45 – 1:45 PM: Lunch

1:45 – 3:00 PM — Plenary 3: Central and South America/Guantanamo

Chair: James Patrick Jordan
Alliance for Global Justice, USA

Speakers:

— **Silvio Platero**, President, MOVPAZ, Cuba
— **Paola Renata Gallo Peláez**, President, MOPASSOL, Argentina
— **Myriam Parada Avila**, Executive Director, School of Peace, Colombia

3:15 – 4:30 PM — Plenary 4: Asia Pacific / Pivot to Asia / Okinawa

Chair: Annette Brownlie
IPAN, Australia

Speakers:

— **Hiroshi Inaba**, Director, Okinawa Peace Support, Okinawa, Japan
— **Tarak Kauf**, Veterans For Peace, USA

4:45 – 6:00 PM — Plenary 5: The Middle East: US/NATO Plan

Chair: MK Aida Touma-Sliman
Peace and Solidarity Committee, Israel

Speakers:

— **Medea Benjamin**, Co-Founder, CODEPINK, USA

— **Richard Boyd Barrett, TD**, Member of Dail Eireann, Ireland
— **Dr. Asad Abushark**, Spokeperson, Great March of Return, Palestine

---

6:00 – 7:30 PM — Dinner

7:30 – 9:00 PM: Cultural Event

Sunday, November 18:

9:00 – 10:15 AM — Plenary 6: Europe / Expansion of NATO

Chair: David Swanson
World BEYOND War, USA

Speakers:

— **Ilda Figueiredo**, Chair, Conselho Português para a Paz e Cooperação, Portugal
— **Frank Keoghan**, Chair, People's Movement, Ireland
— **Jeannie Toschi Marazzani Visconti,** Cominato No Guerra No NATO, Italy

10:30 AM – 1:45 AM — Plenary 7: Africa /AFRICOM

Chair: Margaret Kimberley
UNAC, Black Agenda Report, USA

Speakers:

— **Chris Matlhako**, Coordinator, South Africa Peace Initiative, South Africa
— **Ann Atambo**, President, WILPF Kenya
— **Paul Pumphrey**, Friends of the Congo, USA

11:45 – 12:45 PM: Lunch

12:45–2:00 PM — Regional Organizing Breakout Meetings

— Discussing Regional Plans of Action
— Regional Report Back to the Final Plenary

2:15–3:30 PM — Plenary 8: Global Campaign's Future Plan of Action

Chairs: Roger Cole, PANA, Ireland
Bahman Azad, CAUSFMB, USA

— Identifying Major Campaign Areas
— Planning our actions for the coming year
— Selection of the Coordinating Committee for the Global Campaign
Against US/NATO Military Bases

3:30 – 3:45 PM — Closing Remarks

Monday, November 19:

9:00 AM — Travelling to Shannon for an Anti-Base Demonstration (2:30 hours ride)

Keynote Speakers

Dr. Aledia Guevara, Cuba

Aleida Guevara March is the daughter of Che Guevara and Aleida March. She is a pediatrician at William Soler Children's Hospital in Havana and teaches at the Escuela Latina-Americana de Medicina and at a primary school for children with disabilities. She is the author of several scientific papers published in specialized magazines in Cuba and has presented at various conferences on issues of Public Health in Cuba and on other Cuban issues in Germany, Argentina, Brazil, Cyprus, Ecuador, Spain, France, Greece, India, Italy and Portugal, among other countries. She is the author of a book titled *Chavez, Venezuela and the New Latin America*.

Aengus Ó Snodaigh, TD, Ireland

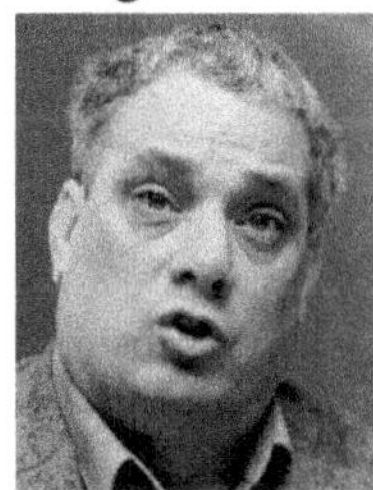

Aengus Ó Snodaigh is currently the Sinn Féin Party Whip in the Dáil and is spokesperson on Social Protection. He was previously the Sinn Féin representative on the National Forum on Europe and the Party's spokesperson on the Treaty of Nice. He was a member of the Dáil Committee on Procedures and Privileges and the Committee on European Affairs in the 29th Dáil. He was re-elected at the 2016 general election. He has been a member of the Sinn Féin national executive, the Ard Chomhairle, for many years; has been on the Dublin executive of the party since 1985; and was part of the Party's negotiations team during the Northern Ireland peace process.

Clare Daly, TD, Ireland

Clare Daly is an independent socialist TD for Dublin Fingal. She was elected to the Dáil in 2011 and in 2016. Clare has been a strong campaigner on many national issues such as the Together for Yes campaign and the Right2Water. In 2014 she along with Deputy Mick Wallace was arrested for attempting to gain access to a military aircraft at Shannon airport in order to prove once and for all the presence of military weapons on aircraft passing through Ireland.

Plenary Speakers

Dr. Asad Abushark

Dr. Asad Abushark is a retired professor of linguistics, a Palestinian human rights activist, and international spokesperson for the Great March of Return. He is from the Gaza Strip and is currently living in Ireland.

Grigoris Anagnostou

Grigoris Anagnostou is a member of the National Council and Organizing Secretary of the Greek Committee for International Detente and Peace (EEDYE). He is a former member of the board of student union (at the University of Ioannina and at the Athens School of Fine Arts). Born in Arta (Northwestern Greece) in 1988, he studied Physics at the University of Ioannina and History of Art at the Athens School of Fine Arts. He has worked as an Art Historian since 2014. He lives in Athens.

Anne Atambo

Anne Atambo is the founder and President of the Women's International League for Peace and Freedom, Kenya. She is a women's rights activist and believes women in Africa are key in reshaping the future of Africa and more importantly, to ensuring sustainable peace and development takes root in the continent. As an advocate of peace, Anne believes that security underpins how women contribute to the community. In this regard, Anne has launched the Peace Labs Project and the Kenyan Women's Voices Podcast and her goal is to involve more women at the grassroots and beyond to decry chaos, conflict and war.

Dr. Bahman Azad

Bahman Azad is a member of the Executive Board and the Organizational Secretary of the U.S. Peace Council, and an NGO representative of the World Peace Council at the United Nations. He serves as the Coordinator of the Coalition Against U.S. Foreign Military Bases and is a member of the Coordinating Committees of the Hands Off Syria Coalition and the United National Antiwar Coalition. He is also the Chair of Iran Working Group of Veterans For Peace. Bahman's area of research also includes the political economy of Capitalism and Socialism. He is the author of the book: *Heroic Struggle, Bitter Defeat: Factors Contributing to the Dismantling of the Socialist State in the USSR.*

Ajamu Baraka

Ajamu Baraka was the Green Party candidate for vice president of the United States in 2016, and serves on the boards of the Center for Constitutional Rights, Africa Action, Latin American Caribbean Community Center, Diaspora Afrique, and the Mississippi Workers' Center for Human Rights. He is the co-founder and National Coordinator of Black Alliance for Peace. From 2004 to 2011, Baraka was the founding executive director of the US Human Rights Network, a nonprofit dedicated to strengthening human rights standards in the United States. Baraka was honored in 1998 by UN Secretary General Kofi Annan as one of 300 human rights defenders brought to Paris to commemorate the signing of the Universal Declaration of Human Rights.

Richard Boyd Barett, TD

Richard Boyd Barrett is People Before Profits TD for Dun Laoghaire Co., Dublin. He is a founder member of the Irish Anti- war movement and one of the principal organisers of the 100,000 strong demonstration in Dublin on February 15th 2003 against the planned US- led war on Iraq and the use of Shannon airport by the US military.

Medea Benjamin

Medea Benjamin is the co-founder of the women-led peace group CODEPINK and the co-founder of the human rights group Global Exchange. She has been an advocate for social justice for more than 40 years. Described as "one of America's most committed -- and most effective — fighters for human rights" by New York Newsday, and "one of the high profile leaders of the peace movement" by the Los Angeles Times, she was one of 1,000 exemplary women from 140 countries nominated to receive the Nobel Peace Prize on behalf of the millions of women who do the essential work of peace worldwide.

Annette Brownlie

Annette Brownlie is the Chairperson of Independent and Peaceful Australia Network (IPAN) and Vice President of the United Nations Association of Australia Queensland Branch and on the committee of Just Peace. Just Peace is the Brisbane organisation formed by a small number of people in 2001 post 9/11 which grew and played a strong role in building community opposition to the wars in Afghanistan Iraq and the continuing support from Australia for the wars in the Middle East.

Roger Cole

Roger Cole was on the National Executive of Irish CND throughout the 1980s. He is Chair and one of the founders of the Peace & Neutrality Alliance in 1996. He was Chief Steward of the protest against President Reagan's visit to Ireland in 1984, and also Chief Steward and one on the main organisers of the protest in Dublin against the Iraq war in 2003. As Chair of PANA, he opposed the Amsterdam, Nice and Lisbon referendums, thus playing a key role in advocating Irish neutrality and opposing the transformation of the EU into an EU Empire with its own Army. He organised one of the first protests against the use of Shannon Airport. He is an Irish Republican.

Moara Crivelente

Moara Crivelente is a member of the Executive Board of the Brazilian Center for Solidarity with the Peoples and Struggle for Peace (CEBRAPAZ), a member organization of the WPC Secretariat. She is a political scientist and journalist engaged in anti-colonialist and anti-imperialist movements, currently conducting Ph.D. research on the Palestinian and Sahrawi struggles for self-determination. She maintains a column at Portal Vermelho, a Brazilian news website, and contributes to other publications with opinion pieces and reports on international politics and the peoples' resistance and struggles against the planet's militarization and war, and for liberation and peace.

Pat Eleder

Pat Elder is a member of the coordinating committee of World Beyond War, the author of *Military Recruiting in the United States*, and the Director of the National Coalition to Protect Student Privacy. Elder was a co-founder of the DC Antiwar Network and a member of the Steering Committee of the National Network Opposing the Militarization of Youth. Pat has crafted bills and helped to pass legislation in Maryland and New Hampshire to curtail recruiter access to student data. He worked to pressure the UN's Committee on the Rights of the Child to call on the Obama Administration to adhere to the Optional Protocol to the Convention on the Rights of the Child on the Involvement of Children in Armed Conflict regarding military recruiting practices in the schools.

Ilda Figueiredo

Ilda Figueiredo is the Chairperson of the National Board of the Portuguese Council for Peace and Cooperation (CPPC), an elected local councilor in the city of Porto, and an economist. She was, for over twelve years, a Member of the European Parliament where she participated in several international liaison committees with Latin America and Asia.

Dr. Margaret Flowers

Margaret Flowers, M.D., is co-director of Popular Resistance, where she organized the Peace Congress to End U.S. Wars at Home and Abroad. Active on a broad range of issues for economic, racial and environmental justice and peace, Flowers is best known for her activism for a single payer national health insurance. Flowers co-hosts Clearing the FOG, a weekly podcast, with Kevin Zeese, and her writing appears regularly in outlets such as Truthdig, Counterpunch and Dissident Voice. She is a national co-chair of the Green Party U.S. and ran for the U.S. Senate in 2016.

Socorro Gomes

Socorro Gomes is the President of the World Peace Council and was most recently reelected in the 2016 World Peace Assembly. She was the President of the Brazilian Center for Solidarity with the Peoples and Struggle for Peace (CEBRAPAZ) and is currently a member of its Advisory Board. She was also a councilwoman and a federal deputy for four terms in Brazil, a secretary of Justice and Human Rights in the government of the Brazilian Federal State of Pará, where she also led the Regional Labor Department.

Fulvio Grimaldi

Fulvio Grimaldi been working as a professional journalist and war correspondent since 1962, for BBC World Service London and Rai-TG3 Italian National Public Television; and for newspapers and magazines like Paese Sera, Giorni-Vie Nuove, ABC, Lotta Continua, Liberazione, The Middle East (London), and New African (London). He left the Italian Public TV service in 1999 over differences regarding NATO's aggression on Serbia. He has been working on international affairs against Western main-stream media distortions and manipulation, producing books and films on the progressive movements in Latin America. He is a member of the National Italy-Cuba Friendship Association and of the Italian Anti-Nato grouping "Lista No NATO."

Dr. Ed Horgan

Dr. Edward Horgan served twenty-two years as an officer in the Irish Defence Forces. He experienced war as a UN peacekeeper in Middle East and experienced reality as senior prison officer. He has worked on twenty-one election missions in post conflict situations in Eastern Europe, the Middle East, Asia, and Africa. He completed a doctoral thesis on Reform of United Nations. Currently he is the Chairperson VFP Ireland, International Secretary Irish Peace and Neutrality Alliance, and peace activist with Shannonwatch. He took a high court constitutional case against the Irish Government over the US military use of Shannon airport. He worked for eight years with a large multinational company causing major pollution. Dr. Horgan tried but failed to arrest G. W. Bush at Shannon airport (mea culpa).

Hiroshi Inaba

Born on the mainland of Japan, Hiroshi Inaba became a resident of Henoko in Okinawa. He is the executive director of "Okinawa Peace Support," a General Incorporated Association based in Henoko. He was arrested in 2016 during a non-violent protest against the construction of a new U.S. military base in Henoko. The case has been appealed to the Japanese Supreme Court. In 2018 he launched a multi-language website "StandWithOkinawa" in English, Chinese, Korean and Japanese to spread updated information on Henoko globally.

James Patrick Jordan

James Patrick Jordan is National Co-Coordinator for the Alliance for Global Justice and AfGJ's representative to the People's Human Rights Observatory (Observatorio de Derechos Humanos del Pueblo). He is responsible for AfGJ's labor, ecology, and Colombia solidarity programs. James studied religion at North Park University, but spent most his working life as a landscaper. He developed as an activist participating in the ecology, labor, and anti-war movements in Tucson, Arizona (US), where he has lived since 1983.

Tarak Kauf

Tarak Kauff was a paratrooper in the U.S. Army for most of his three and a half years in the military. He was discharged in 1962 and has been staunchly opposed to US wars and militarism ever since. He was a Veterans For Peace National Board member for close to six years and has organized and participated in four veterans delegations to Okinawa, two to Palestine, one to Jeju Island, South Korea, and many resistance actions in the U.S. He is also the managing editor of *Peace in Our Times*, VFP's quarterly newspaper. He is on the Executive Committee of the Coalition Against U.S. Foreign Military Bases.

Frank Keoghan

Frank Keoghan is Secretary of the People's Movement in Ireland. He is General President of Connect Trade Union and National Coordinator of the Irish Trade Union Federation. He is also the editor of the biweekly newsletter, *People's News*.

Margaret Kimberley

Margaret Kimberley is Editor and Senior Columnist at Black Agenda Report. She is a regular guest on radio and internet talk shows and has appeared on Al Jazeera English, RT, WBAI, KPFK, Presstv Iran, and Govorit Moskva (Moscow Voice Radio). Ms. Kimberley serves on the Administrative Committee of the United National Antiwar Coalition (UNAC), the Coordinating Committee of Black Alliance for Peace and the Advisory Board of ExposeFacts.org. She is writing a book about racism and the American presidency. She is a graduate of Williams College and lives in New York City.

Milan Krajca

Milan Krajca is a chairman of the Czech Peace Movement. He was one of the organizers of the successful popular movement against efforts to build a US military base in the Czech Republic. Today he organizes activities against US/NATO military presence in the Czech Republic and the Central and Eastern Europe. He is active in the World Peace Council as well as in solidarity campaigns with socialist Cuba and occupied Palestine. He is also a journalist oriented on foreign and international policy. Last year he received the Jan Sverma Journalist Price of the Czech Journalist Association.

Dr. John Lannon

John Lannon is a founding member of Shannonwatch, whose primary focus is ending US military use of the civilian airport at Shannon, Ireland. He has been actively involved in human rights and anti-war campaigning for over two decades. He is a member of the national executive of PANA (Peace and Neutrality Alliance), and is also actively involved in initiatives to support refugees and asylum seekers in Ireland. John works as a lecturer and researcher at the University of Limerick, and has published several academic works in the fields of human rights and development.

Joe Lombardo

Joe Lombardo is a life-long antiwar and labor activist. He is the Co-Coordinator of the United National Antiwar Coalition (UNAC). He is a life-long union member, a member of the Civil Service Employees Association (CSEA) and the Troy Area Labor Council. Joe was a staff person for the National Peace Action Coalition, one of the two major antiwar coalitions in the US that organized against the Vietnam War. He has appeared as a commentator on a number of news outlets and he is the author of many articles on peace and social justice topics.

Mairead Maguire

Mairead Maguire is the recipient of the 1976 Nobel Peace Prize. She is a peace activist from Northern Ireland who co-founded, with Betty Williams and Ciaran McKeown, the Women for Peace, which later became the Community for Peace People, an organization dedicated to encouraging a peaceful resolution of the Troubles in Northern Ireland. In recent years, she has criticised the Israeli government's policy towards Gaza, in particular to the naval blockade. In June 2010, Maguire went on board the MV Rachel Corrie as part of a flotilla that unsuccessfully attempted to breach the blockade.

Alfred L. Marder

Alfred Marder is the President of the U.S. Peace Council and Vice President of the World Peace Council. He is the Honorary President of the International Association of Peace Messenger Cities and NGO Representative at the United Nations. Al is also a member of City of New Haven Peace Commission, President of Amistad Committee, Inc., and Chairman of State of Connecticut's USA Freedom Trail Committee. His Awards include: Mexico Legion of Honor; Government of Sierra Leone, Honor of the Rokal; Medal of Peace, Cuban Moviemento de la Paz; Honor, Union of Dominican Journalists for Peace; Communist Party of Russia; State of Connecticut, USA. He is a Veteran of World War II, Bronze Star.

Chris Matlhako

Chris Matlhako is president of the South African Peace Initiative (SAPI), the 2nd Deputy General of the South African Communist Party (SACP) and former international relations secretary of the Party. He is also the General-Secretary of the Friends of Cuba Society — South Africa, a solidarity movement with Cuba. He has written extensively on international issues and development science postgraduate at the University of the Free State. Serves on the WPC secretariat and Working Group of the International Communist and Workers Parties Meeting (IMCWP).

Dr. Zuhal Okuyan

Zuhal Okuyan is the chairwoman of Peace Committee of Turkey, which was formerly named Peace Association. She is a medical doctor and public health specialist. She teaches part time in a program called 'Human Society and Planet' to the medical school students, which is mainly based on public health and medical ethics issues. She has worked in various NGOs related to health, environment, human rights and local development. She lives in Izmir, Turkey.

Myriam Parada Avila

Myriam Parada Avila is the Director and Founder of the Colombian School of Peace Foundation. She is a trainer and worker in the culture of peace (identity, liberty and respect for human rights); a pacifist dedicated to the struggles of oppressed peoples and to the defense of world peace. Myriam has worked with the Secretary of Education of the District of Bogotá D.C. for the past thirty-eight years, and is an active member of administrative work committees of the Secretary of Education. In 2015, she received recognition from this organization for her commitment to peace and development work with children. Myriam has been a trade union director and leader for more than 15 years.

Silvio Platero

Silvio Platero is the President of MOVPAZ. Silvio has taught it as a professor in Italy. He is the president of the Cuban Movement for Peace and Sovereignty of the Nation. He is also a member of the Executive Committee of WPC and its secretariat. He is the author of books like: *Religious Fundamentalism in the 20th Century* and *New Religious Movements in the Caribbean*. Annually, he organizes international seminars about the abolition of international military bases and about challenges faced by Latin America as a peace zone.

Paul Pumphrey

Paul Anthony Pumphrey has been an organizer and activist for over fifty years. In 2004, Mr. Pumphrey became a co-founding member of the board of directors of Friends of the Congo (FOTC) and its treasurer. FOTC is a non-profit human rights advocacy and information organization focused on justice for the people of the Democratic Republic of the Congo. In 1998, Mr. Pumphrey co-founded Brothers and Sisters International (BASI) as a non-profit organization whose focus is economic development and human rights in the Americas, the Caribbean and Africa.

Paola Renata Gallo Peláez

Paola Renata Gallo Peláez is a lawyer who graduated from the University of Caldas in Colombia, validated by the University of La Plata in Argentina. She specializes in Social Security Law. She is the Co-Chair of the Movement for Peoples' Peace, Sovereignty, and Solidarity (MOPASSOL) in Spanish). She also serves as Co-Director of the Chair for the Peace "Rina Bertaccini," and Chair of the Debate Meetings of the Argentinian-Cuban Fraternity, an organization that seeks to achieve the integration of America (EFAC in Spanish). She holds a master's degree in National Defense Studies from the Argentine University of National Defense (former EDENA in Spanish).

Senator Grace O'Sullivan

Senator Grace O'Sullivan is an ecologist, environmentalist and the Green Party member of Seanad Eireann [Irish Senate] and member of the Seanad Civil Engagement Group. She is the party spokesperson on Marine and Tourism. Grace is a former activist on Greenpeace vessels, including the Rainbow Warrior, and was the Ireland's first female Irish national surf champion. She was the winner of the 2017 Green Leader Award.

Dr. Stelios Sofocli

Dr. Stelios Sofocli is a member of the General Board, and since July 2017 Chairman of the Pan Cyprian Peace Council. During 1983-2008 he was a member of the Board of the District Council and Secretariat of the Progressive Party of Working People (AKEL). He is currently a member of the Central Committee of AKEL. He has a Ph.D. degree in Civil Engineering from the Bauhaus University Weimar/ Germany. He has participated in different missions of the World Peace Council in Palestine, Germany, United Kingdom, Greece and Turkey.

David Swanson

David Swanson is an author, activist, journalist, and radio host. He is director of WorldBeyondWar.org and campaign coordinator for RootsAction.org. Swanson's books include *War Is A Lie* and *When the World Outlawed War*. He blogs at DavidSwanson.org and WarIsACrime.org. He hosts Talk Nation Radio. He is a 2015, 2016, 2017 Nobel Peace Prize Nominee. David's books on war and peace include *War Is A Lie; War Is Never Just*; and *When the World Outlawed War*; as well as (co-author) *A Global Security System: An Alternative to War* (a vision of a world of nonviolent institutions). He hosts a weekly radio show called Talk Nation Radio.

Dr. Aqel Taqz

Dr. Aqel Taqz is the Secretary of the Palestinian Committee for Peace and Solidarity (PCPS), Member of the Secretariat of the World Peace Council, and Coordinator of the WPC's Middle East region. ***He was denied an entry visa by the Irish Government.***

MK Aida Touma-Sliman

A 2007 Nobel Peace Prize nominee, Aida Touma-Sliman is a member of the Israeli Parliament (the Knesset) from the Joint List – Hadash (Democratic Front for Peace and Equality). She is also the Chairwoman of the Knesset's Standing Committee on the Status of Women and Gender Equality — the first Palestinian MK to occupy such a position in Israel. From 2011-15, she was the Chief Editor of *Al-Ittihad*, the only Arabic newspaper published in Israel, and is a co-founder and member of International Women Commission for Just Peace Israel Palestine. Aida Touma-Sliam is currently a Member of the Political Bureau and Central Committee of the Communist Party of Israel. She is also President of Peace and Solidarity Committee in Israel.

Iraklis Tsavaridis

Iraklis Tsavdaridis is the Executive Secretary of the World Peace Council. He joined the Communist Youth of Greece in 1982 and has been a member of the Communist Party of Greece (KKE) since 1985. In 1999, he was elected President of the World Federation of Democratic Youth (WFDY) and served for four years untill 2003. In 2003 he joined the Greek Committee for International Détente and Peace (EEDYE), of which he still is member of the National Secretariat. He has attended hundreds of congresses and conferences worldwide and speaks several languages (Greek, English, German, Spanish and Portugese).

Dr. Dave Webb

Dr. Dave Webb is the Chair of the UK Campaign for Nuclear Disarmament. He is an Emeritus Professor of Engineering who switched subjects and departments to become Professor of Peace and Conflict Studies at Leeds Beckett University in the UK. He retired in 2012 to focus on peace campaigning. He is also Convener of the Global Network board of directors, a Vice-President of the International Peace Bureau, a board member of Abolition 2000 and a patron of the UK group Scientists for Global Responsibility.

Lucas Wirl

Lucas Wirl studied Sociology, Peace and Conflict Studies, and Anglistics at the University of Marburg, Germany. Interning with Peace Action Wisconsin (USA) in 2008, he continued working in the peace movement. Today, he is executive director of the International Association of Lawyers Against Nuclear Arms (IALANA), co-chair of the international coordinating committee of the international network No to War – No to NATO, program director of the International Network of Engineers and Scientists for Global Responsibility (INES), as well as council member of the International Peace Bureau (IPB). Furthermore, Lucas Wirl is actively engaged in the struggle for a peaceful orientation of universities (Civil Clause), the campaign Stop Air Base Ramstein, and the German campaign "Disarmament Instead of Armament."

Hiroji Yamashiro

Hiroji Yamashiro is Chairman of the Okinawa Peace Action Center. Born in Okinawa in 1952, he received his BA degree in sociology from Hosei University. In 1982, he joined the Okinawa prefectural government, dealing with employee issues of USFJ (United States Forces Japan) in Okinawa, the disposal of unexploded bombs and at the revenue service department. He also served as vice-chairman of a labor union formed by Okinawa governmental employees. Since 2004, he has been Chairman of the Okinawa Peace Action Center, leading protest actions against the construction of a new U.S. military base in Henoko, as well as the Osprey helipads in Takae in Hi-gashi village. He became a symbolic figure of the non-violent peace movement in Okinawa. Arrested during a confrontation with the riot police in Takae, he was detained for 5 months and found guilty at the district court. He immediately appealed and his legal fight continues.

International Night

Chair: Edward Horgan
Peace and Neutrality Alliance
Ireland

Conference Opening Remarks

Roger Cole
Peace And Neutrality Alliance
Ireland

I welcome everyone to Dublin for the first International Conference Against US/NATO Military Bases, which is being hosted by the Peace and Neutrality Alliance (PANA) on behalf of and in conjunction with the Coalition Against US Foreign Military Bases, USA.

I know we all benefit from the papers we are about to hear and that we will get to know each other better in order to build a global peace movement.

The founder of Irish republicanism, Theobold Wolfe Tone, who was the driving force behind the 1798 rebellion against British rule in Ireland, was the first person to annunciate the principle of Irish neutrality. Tone fought for an Ireland that was an independent, democratic and neutral republic and that was based on equality for all. That tradition continues to this day, which is why PANA is proud to be hosting this important conference. The struggle for Irish freedom was, and remains, part of the struggle for a peaceful world without war, without aggression and without empires.

Chair's Opening Remarks:

Edward Horgan
International Secretary
Peace and Neutrality Alliance
Ireland

This paper will emphasise what we as individuals must do to promote peace, including getting rid of foreign military bases, especially US and NATO bases. There is a Just War Theory that suggests that wars can be just and justified. In modern times with modern weapons of mass destruction, no war can be justified because there is always a peaceful or non-violent alternative, and wars only occur when these alternatives fail to be applied. Some will argue that capital punishment is justified in certain circumstances. Historical experience has shown that a high percentage of those sentenced to death were innocent, and those statistics should mean that capital punishment should be outlawed in all countries, as it is in all European Union countries. However, several EU countries are committing acts of capital punishment by killing thousands of people in air attacks in the unjustified so-called war on terror. The United States has been forced to partly abandon its practice of torturing prisoners of war due to international condemnation, but it has replaced much of its torture program with drone and special forces assassinations, which involve even more serious human rights abuses and gross breaches of international laws. US military bases in the Middle East are used carry out these illegal targeted assassinations.

Human rights abuses occur primarily because of the deliberate actions of the abusers, and killing people is the ultimate and most serious human rights abuse. But human rights abuses, including mass killings, also occur because of the inactions of those who stand idly by, and choose to do nothing. In the past there was a presumption that good would overcome evil in the longer-term, yet others argue that wars, short term self-interest, greed, and man's innate brutal tendencies, will often overcome our better instincts. World Wars 1 and 2 tend to support the power of evil over good, but only if we forget that in the modern media good news is no news and we are subjected to a barrage of daily bad news. Regardless of such arguments, humanity is now in a new level of crisis. With the advent of weapons of mass destruction, especially nuclear weapons, combined with the ongoing and increasing environmental damage to our living and survival environment, arguments about good and evil are almost irrelevant. The survival of humanity is at stake. If we fail to overcome the destructive forces that are destroying our societies and our living environment then we, as individuals and humanity, are heading towards extinction. Positively promoting peace, protecting life and opposing war — these are no longer just nice and good ideas, they are essential tools of survival.

In 1914, in spite of a very active peace movement, Europe and the world carelessly and recklessly drifted into the hugely destructive World War I, which arguably did not really end in 1918 — the conflict just paused for two decades and resumed in 1939. A flawed peace agreement is just a temporary ceasefire, without comprehensive reconciliation and atonement by all sides. Humanity is now in my view at a very similar tipping point like 1913, only this time there may be no coming back to peace and normality. World War 1 was promoted as the 'war to end all wars', and this was very clearly just fake news. However, World War 3, if it occurs, may indeed be the war to end all wars, because there may be no one or nothing left at the end of World War 3 to fight World War 4. Just as World War 1 was unnecessary and avoidable, and if World War 1 had been avoided then Word War 2 could also have been avoided, likewise World War 3 is avoidable, and the tools for avoiding World War 3 include actively promoting peace, combined with human ingenuity.

Human ingenuity has given us weapons of mass destruction, destructive neoliberal capitalism, slavery, colonialism, neocolonialism, racism, all designed to enable the powerful elites in our societies and our countries to achieve a hugely undue share of the world's resources at the expense of the vast majority of humanity. The propaganda we are exposed to in the Western media is far more effective than the propaganda used by Reich Minister of Propaganda, Joseph Goebbels. It extolls the false virtues of war mongers such as John McCain, and denigrates peace activists as troublesome utopian unrealistic individuals. We as peace activists must use our ingenuity and actively engage in peace propaganda, but unlike Joseph Goebbels and Donald Trump, our peace propaganda must be based on truth, justice and ingenuity.

Our Western politicians cynically speak of American exceptionalism and values, and European civilisation and values. Yes, the very short American history has been exceptional in all the wrong ways since Amerigo Vespucci brought European invaders, genocide, slavery and racism to the continent we now call America. European values and so-called civilization included slavery, genocide, colonialism, and even today, destructive neo-colonialism and resource wars.

Human agency — what humans do and don't do — is a matter of what human individuals do or fail to do, as distinct from what large organisations such as governments, states, international organisations such as the UN, or religious groups do. It is individuals within these organisations who take action, or fail to take action. It was not the Nazi regime that perpetrated the Holocaust and World War 2. The Nazi regime coordinated it but it was tens of thousands or millions of individuals in Germany and in many other European countries that perpetrated these actions, or allowed these actions to happen by failing to take appropriate actions to prevent or stop the Holocaust or World War 2. Likewise if World War 3 happens, it will be individuals like you and I who either cause it happen, or who fail by our inactions to prevent it from happening. Far too many are still obeying orders that should never be obeyed. In the past the Crusades were perpetrated on the peoples of the Middle East by religious and political leaders who abused the powers that they had assumed for themselves, to have their orders obeyed without question. We must use our conscience and intelligence to evaluate the ethics and correctness of all such orders. An example of how this should be applied can be seen in the oath taken by the soldiers of various armies. In most countries soldiers take an oath to obey all orders from their superiors, on the presumption that their superiors are always correct. The oath taken by Irish soldiers, stipulates that they must obey all LAWFUL orders from their superiors. This means that it is unlawful for an Irish soldier to obey an unlawful order, and this is one of the reasons for their very good reputation as United Nations peacekeepers. Oaths of obedience are also taken by many religious orders and in both cases this has led to very serious abuses of human rights, including war crimes and abuses of children by clergy.

In 1973-74 I served as a UN peacekeeper in the Middle East in the Sinai Desert at the end of the Yom Kippur war. Like many other peacekeeping soldiers I was almost killed on a few occasions and eighty-eight Irish soldiers have been killed on UN peacekeeping duties. While such deaths are regrettable, they are justified in the cause of promoting peace, as distinct from waging war. Ireland and the Irish Defence Forces have successfully used Positive Neutrality to promote international peace, and other countries that are now supposedly making peace by making war should follow Ireland's example. Just as the crimes committed in the name of Christianity in the past were an abuse of religion rather than caused by religion, likewise the horrific crimes committed by ISIS and Al Qaeda have been a gross abuse of the Islamic religion. The abuses being committed by Israel against the Palestinian people are also an abuse of the Jewish religion. 'You shall not kill' is also a commandment of the Jewish religion. The same applies to the abuses being committed by members of the majority Buddhist community in Myanmar against the minority Muslim Rohingya community. In all such cases it is individuals who are committing these crimes, and these crimes are being facilitated by the inactions of many more individuals. The words Yom Kippur stand for A Day of Atonement in the Jewish religion. All religions and all countries should consider introducing days of atonement and genuine acts of atonement, reparation and reconciliation.

Humanity is now facing a coming together or confluence of crises that could destroy humanity and our living environment on this very vulnerable Planet Earth.

The existing or impending crises in possible order of priority include:
1. The real risk of nuclear war
2. Climate change and catastrophic damage to our environment
3. Unjustified conventional wars causing millions of deaths, infrastructural and environmental damage
4. The resulting refugee and migrant crisis
5. The economic chaos being caused by destructive neo-liberal global economic systems
6. Political upheaval across the world.

1. The real risk of nuclear war:

World War 1 and World War 2 were dreadful and avoidable catastrophes. However, it was not until the US dropped atomic bombs on Hiroshima and Nagasaki that humanity achieved the capacity to utterly destroy itself and all of its living environment. That risk has not lessened with the end of the Cold War, and it has increased significantly in the past few years with irresponsible leadership in many Western countries. It is not just Donald Trump and Kim Jong-un that we need worry about. Our neighbours, Britain and France, also have stockpiles of nuclear weapons and probable policies of first use of these nuclear bombs, and the manner in which Russia is being unjustifiably encircled and threatened economically and militarily is a recipe for nuclear disaster.

2. Climate change and catastrophic damage to our environment:

While nuclear war is a possibility, climate change and disastrous damage to our living environment is not only likely it has already occurred and the damage is increasing exponentially. Human ingenuity is capable of reversing most of this damage provided we do not allow it to reach a point of no return, which we are approaching. Small improvements like getting rid of plastic packaging and recycling some materials are no longer adequate. We now need urgent major environmental projects, including banning nuclear power and weapons, ending the use of fossil fuels, restoring our forests in large areas of the planet, cleaning up and protecting our seas and the marine life, protecting our agricultural lands from soil erosion and from damage by pesticides and herbicides. We have the technology and the resources and the ingenuity, but we need to use them now before it is too late.

3. Unjustified conventional wars causing millions of deaths and infrastructural and environmental damage:

The global Military Industrial Complex (MIC), has grown to be more powerful than even the Government of the United States, and instead of taking its orders and instructions from the various governments the MIC is dictating foreign and war policies for the benefit of arms industries and the benefit of those who benefit from wars. Neutral countries such as Switzerland, Ireland, Sweden, Finland and Austria are being threatened if they do not go along with the wishes of the war mongers. NATO's so-called Partnership for Peace, which now includes all these neutral countries, is simply an attempt to drag these countries into the NATO alliance and make us complicit in their war crimes. It is a Partnership for War, not a Partnership for Peace. In each of these countries there are individuals and groups who have vested interests in wars, under the false guise of Humanitarian Intervention, as the people of the former Yugoslavia know to their cost.

The overthrow of the Libyan Government in 2011 is one of the more dreadful examples. The NATO attack on Libya in 2011 launched over 14,000 air attacks on Libya. Nineteen states were involved in this so-called humanitarian operation misusing an unjustified UN Security Council resolution. These countries included EU states Belgium, Denmark, France, Italy, Spain, UK, Bulgaria, Greece, Netherlands, Romania, in all of which capital punishment is outlawed, as well as Canada, Norway, Qatar, US, Jordan, and the United Arab Emirates. Denmark dropped 107 so-called precision bombs on Libya. Neutral Sweden, not to be denied the opportunity to miss out on demonstrating and selling their fighter jets and weapons, joined in and provided eight fighter jets in support of the NATO mission. Peace-loving Norway dropped nearly 600 bombs on Libya, all of course in the supposed interests of bring peace, freedom, human rights and democracy to Libya. We have seen in the meantime how well these spurious objectives have been achieved.

It was not just the fighter pilots who dropped these bombs that were responsible for these war crimes. It was the individual citizens of these countries who failed to prevent their governments from unjustifiably attacking the peoples of countries such as Libya, Afghanistan, Iraq, Syria and Yemen. Of course peaceful neutral Ireland would never participate in such dreadful behaviour, would it? During all these wars since 1999, including the NATO war against Yugoslavia, the neutral Irish Government allowed the US military to use Shannon airport as a refuelling stop for thousands of US military aircraft, in gross breach of international law on neutrality. Three million armed US troops have travelled through Shannon airport, and tens of thousands of aircraft associated with the US military have been refuelled at Shannon.

4. The resulting refugee and migrant crisis:

The victims of these wars and economic abuses are fleeing across the Mediterranean, and we are now refusing to pick them up and are letting them drown in large numbers. Those few we do rescue we are now sending back to dreadful concentration camps in Libya, where gross human rights abuses, including slavery and sexual abuse, are rampant, and to other countries that we have already destroyed. We should begin by changing the missions or orders our countries give to our naval services that were initially being used to genuinely rescue these drowning migrants. Now their role has been changed to sinking the smugglers' boats, and transporting those few that we do pick up out of the sea back to Libya. Our European Governments have taken a positive decision to stop rescuing migrants from the Mediterranean and this is not just unethical, it is in clear breach of international law of the sea; it is a crime against humanity. Genuine humanitarian rescue ships are being denied access to ports in the European Union to deliver the migrants they have rescued. This is truly shameful. If the word Ethics means anything — it must mean that we cannot allow thousands of innocent people fleeing from wars, human rights abuses and gross poverty – to drown before our eyes in the Mediterranean. Of course it is easy to avert our eyes and pretend we don't see them drowning. We can behave like the three monkeys, seeing no evil, hearing no evil and speaking no evil.

5. The economic chaos being caused by destructive neoliberal global economic systems:

This economic chaos may not seem very real here in prosperous Europe. However if we step out of the privileged bubbles that we live in and walk through the back streets of Cairo, Jakarta and Kinshasa, and other even poorer countries, as I have, we realise or should realise that our privileged bubbles are at the expense of these poorer societies. Kinshasa and the Congo are good or dreadful examples. The Congo is probably the richest country in the world from a resources point of view, but its people are among the poorest and the most exploited. It is we Europeans who have exploited and are still exploiting such countries and their peoples. Davos in Switzerland is not just a nice ski resort. It is also where the elite of the world meet each year at the World Economic Forum to plot and ensure that their group remain the elite at the expense of everyone else.

6. Political upheaval across the world:

Political upheaval across the world has resulted in right-wing, left-wing and religious fundamentalist groups destroying our existing political and social systems. Our political and social systems are not perfect, they never will be, and we must always be working to update and improve our governance systems. However, over the past few years far from improving our social and governance systems, there has been very significant deterioration and damage to our governance systems. The rule of law at international level has been abandoned. The UN Charter has been virtually torn up. It is no longer dictators such as Saddam Hussein, Muammar Gaddafi, or Idi Amin who are the biggest threat to humanity, but some of the democratically elected leaders in Western countries. These are our democratic countries, and our leaders, and it is our responsibility to hold our leaders to account.

We individuals are almost brainwashed by governments and other large organisations into believing that we individuals are almost powerless to do anything to prevent these organisations, or the individuals who control and benefit from these organisations, from doing what they want to do, regardless of the destruction they are causing. The so-called military industrial complex includes NATO, which is by far its most powerful and most damaging part. A European Union Army officially does not yet exist, but the recent Permanent Structured Cooperation (PESCO) developments are clearly intended to create a real and powerful additional European army. The last thing humanity needs is another large army, to further destroy our environment.

It is vital that we as individuals understand that we are not powerless and that we can and must take action to prevent our world, our civilization and our very vulnerable living environment being destroyed. We can also achieve results at times by inactions – such as refusing to cooperate with the destructive plans of destructive organisations, refusing to serve in unjustified wars, refusing to be the equivalent of the stationmasters who helped by obeying orders to transport millions of people to the Holocaust death camps.

We are here today in a nice relaxed cordial atmosphere, yet the Barbarians are at the gates. And the Barbarians are not the usual hoards coming from the East wielding swords. Genghis Khan and the Soviet Union no longer exist. Today's Barbarians are coming from the West, coming from within our own democratic countries and wielding so-called smart bombs fired from unmanned drones. We must take urgent action now.

The International Conference Against US/NATO Military Bases in Dublin was supported by a wide range of peace and anti-war organisations. However, the success of this important conference and the prospects for building on this success rests primarily with all the dedicated individuals who organised and participated and networked to make this conference such a huge success.

There are very many reasons why we should oppose military bases, promote peace and campaign against wars. However, one of the most basic reasons for opposing modern wars is that with modern military weapons and modern methods of making war, especially by the United States and its allies including NATO, tens of thousands of children are recklessly killed in these wars. I am involved in a project called naming the children that is attempting to name and commemorate in appropriate ways as many of the children as possible who have been killed or who have died as a result of US-led wars in the Middle East since the first Gulf War in 1991 (*www.namingthechildren.com*). Our estimate is that up to one million children have died as a result of these wars. Children by definition are totally Innocent victims of such wars and their deaths are inexcusable, and amount to crimes against humanity.

For many in our privileged Western societies these dead children are just Collateral Damage, resulting from a so-called War on Terror in faraway places. Far too many consider it none of their business.

I will finish by listing just a small sample of the names of some of these dead children from some of the countries we have so far included in our list. I will begin with those children killed by acts of terror in Western countries, and then include some from the very many more killed by acts of terror, include state and NATO terrorism, across the Middle East and parts of Africa.

In the attack on New York that was wrongfully used to justify the war on terror, one Irish child, Juliana Clifford McCourt, was killed when the plane she was on was crashed into the Twin Towers in New York in an unjustified act of terror. Seven other children were killed in that attack.

— Ireland, New York, 9 Sept 2011, Juliana Clifford McCourt age 4.
— France, Nice, 14 July 2016, Léana Sahraoui, age 2
— Germany, Munich, 22 July 2016, Sabina Sulaj, age 14
— Spain, Barcelona, 17th August 2017, Julian Cadman, age 7
— Britain, Manchester, 22nd May 2017, Saffie Rose Roussos, age 8
— Afghanistan, Afghanistan air strike: UN confirms 30 child deaths in April attack 2018
— Yemen, Asma Fahad Ali al Ameri, age 3 months, January 2016
— Syria, Maher al-Tarni, Aleppo, 26 April 2017
— Palestine, 3 August, 2014, Maria Mohammed Abu Jazar, age 2, Rafah, and her twin brother Firas Mohammed Abu Jazar, age 2 Rafah, 3 August, 2014

— Israel, 6 March 2008, Segev Peniel Avihail Hashahar, Jerusalem, age 15. 2,149 Palestinian children and 134 Israeli children have been killed since September 29, 2000.
— Pakistan: Maezol Khan F Drone, age 8
— Iraq: As many as 576,000 Iraqi children may have died since the end of the Persian Gulf War because of economic sanctions imposed by the UN Security Council.

US Secretary of State, Madeline Albright, once asked General Colin Powell, "what is the point of having such a great army, if we don't use it". When questioned about the Iraqi sanctions and whether it was worth the deaths of over half a million Iraqi children she replied: "yes, it was worth it".

Let us pause and say a silent prayer for all those children who have died because of these unjustified wars. May they rest in peace, because they certainly were not allowed to live in peace.

The lives of all children are equally precious and we must avoid treating their deaths as just collateral damage. Joseph Stalin is credited with saying that "one man's death is a tragedy — one million deaths is just a statistic". He went on to create many such 'statistics'. A Palestinian child is a precious as an Israeli child, or a Syrian child or a Yemeni child or an Irish child.

The just war theory tells us we must wage war with *Jus ad Bellum* and *Jus in Bello* [the right to war].

There is no justification or justice towards making war, and there is no justification or justice in how war is made.

Let us make peace instead.

Aengus O'Snodaigh, TD
Sinn Féin
Ireland

We are in a building and in a location in Dublin that is very appropriate for this conference. This building houses the largest trade union in Ireland. A century ago James Connolly was one of the leaders of that union. He was a socialist and a republican. After a long and bitter strike in Dublin in 1913 he, with others, founded the Irish Citizen Army, which along with other republican forces, launched the 1916 Rising a short distance from here. He was executed after the Rising sitting on a chair because of the wounds he received during the fighting. James Connolly was also President of the Irish Neutrality League.

Since the 1916 Rising, a lot has happened in this country but the Republic the men and women of 1916 fought for has not been achieved, including in the area of foreign affairs. A lot has happened outside of Ireland too. World War I was meant to be the war to end all wars but of course it wasn't. Indeed today's European elite, assisted by their Irish acolytes, is attempting to exploit the commemoration of WWI to advance the creation of a European army, which is being supported by German Chancellor, Angela Merkel, President Macron of France and Jean-Claude Juncker, the President of the European Commission, among others.

The drive to create a European army is part of a pattern of behaviour by empires and would-be empires — the US, the European Union, the Russians and the Chinese — to wage war to capture and exploit the world's resources thus preventing smaller countries from developing, not to mention in many cases laying waste to such countries. The misery of war is well understood by ordinary people, who bear the brunt of it, but is ignored by the elites, who don't. Their friends in the arms industry do well out of war despite the fact that vast amounts of resources are diverted from productive and useful activities that would benefit mankind into obscene profits for the arms industry.

The history of Ireland is a good example of the effects of war and imperialism on a country and on a people. At the end of the 19th century, Dublin, which was then a city of less than one million people, had twenty British army military bases, not to put down the people (although that was necessary from time to time during our long and difficult history) but mainly to attract cannon fodder for Britain's imperial wars. Perhaps as many as 40,000 Irishmen died in the industrial slaughter of World War I, the ultimate imperialist war. Ireland did not declare war on any other country during WWI. We were not an ally or an enemy of any country during that war. We were, however, a British colony exploited by the imperial power, as colonies always are, for, among things, cannon fodder.

One of the greatest political slogans of the 20th century, which emerged out of the Irish Neutrality League and the efforts to keep this country out of WWI and which was hoisted in a banner from the building on this site that was destroyed in the 1916 Rising, proclaimed that WE SUPPORT NEITHER KING NOR KAISER BUT IRELAND. Today's Irish establishment is trying to subvert that powerful slogan and ideal, which was strongly supported by the Irish people and which propelled Irish Republicans to a famous victory in the UK-wide general election of December 1918 in which they won three quarters of the Irish-based seats in the UK House of Commons. The ideal of Irish neutrality is still strongly supported by the people of this State.

As I said above, the Irish State managed to create some freedom since the struggle for independence a century ago but it is an incomplete freedom. Britain retained three military bases in this State, which Eamon De Valera, then Taoiseach [Prime Minister] and later President of Ireland, won back for the Irish State in 1938 — in the nick of time. The six counties of Northern Ireland, however, remained under British control. N. Ireland indeed was the most militarized place in western Europe for periods of the recent troubles. One heliport in Northern Ireland was the most active military helicopter base in the world for ten straight years during that time. The British are still in Northern Ireland.

Clare Daly will speak about a US military base in this part of Ireland

— Shannon Airport. Irish anti-war activists will continue to oppose the use of Shannon as a US military base. My only regret is that the 100,000 people who took to the streets of Dublin to protest just before the US launched its attack on Iraq in 2003 are not on the streets today demanding that Irish neutrality be respected by the Government, telling the world that Ireland is not a belligerent today any more than it was in WWI or WWII and that we object to the use of Shannon Airport as a US military base.

Go raibh maith agat. [Thank you very much.]

Clare Daly, TD
Dail Eireann
Ireland

I am very glad to have the opportunity to address this conference.

Reading the Unity Statement I was struck, in particular, by two sentences '… Stationed throughout the world, almost 1,000 in number, US/NATO military bases are symbols of the ability of the United States to intrude into the lives of sovereign nations and peoples. … Whether invited in or not by domestic interests that have agreed to be junior partners, no country, no peoples, no government, can claim to be able to make decisions totally in the interest of their people, with foreign troops on their soil representing interests antagonistic to those of their peoples.'

The problem is particularly acute in Ireland. To all intents and purposes we are a vassal state of the United States because of the use of Shannon Airport by the US military. The vassal status is also reflected in our economic policy, in particular through our policy of relying on foreign direct investment (FDI) from the United States. Both are of course linked: the fear of losing US FDI contributed to the decision to open up Shannon Airport to the US military.

It is a testament to the Irish people that they continue, in opinion poll after opinion poll, to support neutrality despite the barrage of propaganda in favour of abandoning it. In this supposedly neutral country, the media and the establishment generally continue to challenge neutrality. There are, nevertheless, forces represented at this conference and elsewhere, including students, trade unions, activists and members of parliament, such as myself, who continue to defend neutrality and to speak out about the fact that Ireland today is facilitating war.

It is important to put this conference in context. The US continues to destabilise the world, including the Yemen, where the suffering of the people is extreme, in the pursuit of profits. In Europe, efforts are being made to create a European army. The German Chancellor, Angela Merkel, has said that unanimity among the Member States of the European Union should not be a requirement to establish a European army. We in Ireland could find ourselves participating in a war of which we want no part.

It is important to mention Shannon Airport in the context of this conference. It has been described by Dr. Tom Clonan, a retired Irish army officer and now a security analyst and academic, as a virtual forward base for the US military. The use of Shannon as a US military base really took off in 2003 during the Iraq war. The Irish Government came under severe pressure to permit the US military to use it despite the fact its use was, and is, in breach of the Hague Convention and Irish neutrality.

We have to be grateful to WikiLeaks and to its founder, Julian Assange, for providing us with information about the interactions between the Irish and US Governments on the use of Shannon Airport. We know from WikiLeaks that the Irish Government, acting in an embarrassing and utterly spineless fashion, begged the US authorities to permit the Irish State to search a few US military aircraft. However, the US authorities said "no" so the Irish authorities continue to peddle the line that they have been given a diplomatic assurance that the aircraft are not carrying military equipment. Meanwhile, hundreds of armed US troops pass through Shannon every day. On 10th October 2018 alone, seven aircraft carrying hundreds of US troops passed through the airport; 61,000 in total in 2017, without a murmur from the media.

I would like to take this opportunity to refer to the plight of Julian Assange, a brave man trying to perform the duties of a journalist in a hostile world. His health is suffering because of the behaviour of the British Government.

The United States is pushing Ireland to see how far we will go. The Government here is pushing the Irish people to see how much we will put up with. As a public representative, I am aware of the disquiet among the public about the use of Shannon Airport by the US military. If, however, the Irish public knew the full story of the scale of the use of Shannon by the US and the fact that the airport is now effectively a US military base they would be horrified. Those of us in Ireland concerned about this issue must do more to inform the public, despite the impediments put in our way, about what has been going on. Sadly, however, not all of the people are on the side of peace and justice. As I have already said, we face a hostile media in Ireland, which has given up any pretence of being anything other than a spokesman for the Government and the establishment. Indeed, one of the issues faced by this conference and by anti-war activists globally is the disconnect between people and elites.

The last British army survivor of World War 1, who died in 2009, said that the politicians should have been given the guns and sent to the front. They initiated the mass industrial-scale slaughter that was WW1. Imperialist wars are always started by elites not by the people, who want peace.

It is a privilege for me as an Irish citizen and as a member of parliament to have had the opportunity to address this conference today. The conference gives us an opportunity to share experiences and to highlight the issues that we confront in the struggle against imperialism and war. This is the most important initiative against war that has taken place in Ireland since the mass demonstrations just before the start of the Iraq war, which, in turn, were the largest since the Vietnam war in the 1960s.

Rome wasn't built in a day but building did begin on one day. The struggle against US and NATO imperialism will last long after this conference is over but it is a privilege to be able to say that we were at the first international conference against US/NATO military bases.

Thank you.

Mairead Maguire
Nobel Peace Laureate
Ireland

Dear Friends,

It is good to be here with you all. I would like to thank the organizers for inviting me to address the conference and to be present to support the call to close all US/NATO Bases. Firstly I thank you for your work for peace. It is good that we will have an opportunity in the next few days to get to know each other and together discuss what kind of a world we want to live in.

There will be many different perspectives on this and the way forward, but let us agree to respect each other and to engage in deep listening and conversation no matter how hard and where the dialogue might take us!

Let us be encouraged by the fact that we have made an important first step when we agree to enter into dialogue, and when we agree that Peace is both the means and the great achievable gift. It would be wonderful too no matter what area of social/political change we work in, if we can unite on a shared vision of a demilitarized world and find strength in agreeing we will not limit ourselves to civilizing and slowing down militarism, but demanding its total abolition.

Some people might argue that Peace is not possible in such a highly militarized world. However, I believe that Peace is both possible and urgent. It is achievable when we each become impassioned about peace and filled with an ethic that makes peace our objective and we each put into practice our moral sense of political/social responsibility to build peace and justice.

To build peace we are challenged to reject the bomb, the bullet and all the techniques of violence. Unfortunately, we are constantly bombarded with the glorification of militarism and war so building a culture of peace and nonviolence will not be an easy task. We are hearing about the building of a European Army and we are asked to accept austerity and budget cuts to our health and education, etc., whilst increasing money to our own armies and also European military expansion.

The North Atlantic Treaty Organization (NATO), which should have been disbanded when the Warsaw Pact was dissolved, continues to carry out wars and proxy wars in many countries, pushing towards the borders of Russia and resurrecting a cold war between East and West. I believe that NATO should be disbanded and should be made accountable and make restitution, to the millions of people in countries such as Afghanistan, Iraq, Libya, and many others it has illegally attacked, invaded and destroyed. We will never be allowed by our Governments, or our mainstream media, to hear the stories of the lives of so many civilians killed by US/NATO forces. NATO forces have targeted and assassinated individuals, and entire families. It is to all our shame in the international community, that their illegal and criminal acts of horror and bloodletting, which embodies the comeback of barbarism, is allowed to continue. NATO should be brought before the International Criminal Court for war crimes.

It would be all too easy to point fingers and play the blame game but unless we all take responsibility for the highly dangerous militarised situation with which we are faced in the world today, things will not get better. Ireland, with the militarization of its Foreign and Defence Policy, I feel has been unfaithful to the Irish peoples' wish for a Neutral State and worse has been complicit by accommodating illegal wars. Ireland's peace activists have been peacefully protesting US military use of Irish airports whereby over two and a half million armed US troops have passed through Shannon airport on their way to and from the US-led Afghan and Iraq wars. I believe Ireland should refuse permission to any further stopover and refueling facilities being granted to aeroplanes ferrying troops or munitions to the wars and should also withdraw Irish participation from all NATO and EU military operations overseas.

Ireland is deeply admired in many countries and has a proud record in helping developing countries. Their role as mediators and peace negotiators is well known. I would like to propose that Ireland disband their Army and focus their finance and people on developing their great expertise in the Science of Peacemaking through a Government Department of Peace.

Re-committing to its tradition of neutrality and multi-lateralism, placing ethics, morality and justice as core values at the heart of its Foreign Policy would send out a clear message of the Irish Government rejecting the road of militarism and war and choosing the road of peace and reconciliation, both locally and internationally.

For Humanity's survival, through a reformed United Nations, we need to move to General and Complete Disarmament — including nuclear weapons. This is not an impossible dream. I commend the Irish Government in their work at the United Nations to work for Nuclear Disarmament. I believe we can take hope from Pope Francis' statement; after pointing out the dangers of nuclear weapons, he says, "the threat of their use, as well as their very possession, is to be firmly condemned."

And the Pope quotes as an example the "historic vote at the UN" where "the majority of the members of the international community determined that nuclear weapons are not only immoral, but also must be considered an illegal means of warfare."

It is to be hoped that the USA, Russia, the UK, Israel and other nuclear armed states will begin to dismantle their nuclear weapons, and help turn back the hands of the doomsday clock. Up to the end of 1961, at the United Nations, general and complete disarmament was the aim of all governments. In a joint Soviet Union-United States statement of 20th September, 1961, they stated:

"The goal of negotiations is to achieve agreement on a programme which will ensure (a) that disarmament is general and complete and war is no longer an instrument for settling international problems."

Let us unite our voices to call for an end to enmity and war, and for President Trump and President Putin to join together with all world leaders in a World Peace Conference to work for an agreed Programme of General and Complete Disarmament. Such courageous leadership towards dialogue and disarmament would give hope to humanity.

Socorro Gomes
President, World Peace Council
Brazil

Dear fellows in charge of organizing this conference and friends from the Peace and Neutrality Alliance, to whom we express our great appreciation for welcoming us,

Dear fellows of the various organizations represented here, those working tirelessly for a broad unity around our common struggle,

It is an honor to greet you in this opportunity on behalf of the World Peace Council.

The dialogue that we hold here is necessary for us to set converging perspectives in a world conjuncture of deepening economic and social problems and political conflicts, one in which the imperialist offensive is intensifying and part of that is its militarist strategy, with NATO's reinforcement and the dissemination of military bases all over the planet. This offensive is particularly sensitive in regions such as Latin America, the Middle East, Africa and Asia.

Our broader and more effective mobilization in resolute opposition to the planet's militarization is more than timely and urgent. The dissemination of US and NATO military bases throughout all continents is a constant threat, part of an offensive policy that can easily escalate to conflicts and culminate in interference, military interventions and aggression, in flagrant violation of nations' sovereignty, trampling over international law in outrageous imposition of generalized suffering on the peoples victimized.

Side by side with various organizations, the World Peace Council promotes firm campaigns against foreign military bases, for NATO's dissolution and for the member nations' right to disengage from this imperialist war machine.

Comrade Silvio Platero, the President of the Cuban Movement for the Peoples' Sovereignty and Peace (MOVPAZ), will surely explain one of our main initiatives, promoted jointly by the World Peace Council, MovPaz and other Cuban organizations: the International Seminar for Peace and the Abolition of Foreign Military Bases.

It is necessary to strengthen our denunciation that the US alone has around 1,000 bases and other military facilities spread throughout the world and that, through NATO, which uses these and other bases such as British, French and Italian, it even harbors nuclear warheads in facilities in countries that are not nuclear powers such as Turkey, Belgium, Italy and the Netherlands, among others, through the so-called nuclear sharing program. We must emphatically reject the abuse of these resources in the framework of what the powers term as "deterrence." This is the powers' strategy of keeping a generalized threat to impose their agenda on the peoples throughout the world.

Another tactic prominently employed in their "deterrence policy," since 1951, is the war exercise, combining the armed forces of member countries and, often, of the military bloc's "partners." Examples are the recently conducted "Saber Strike," (Poland, June 28) led by the US and which mobilized around 18,000 troops from nineteen allies and partners, and "Trident Juncture," which the powers seem the most proud of recently, the biggest military exercise ever undertaken since the end of the Cold War, and which concluded earlier this November in Norway, involving 50,000 troops from over thirty countries.

Besides the disastrous, devastating and criminal interventions in Bosnia-Herzegovina in 1994-1995, the monstrous attack on Yugoslavia in 1999, and against Libya in 2011, NATO intervened in Afghanistan and Iraq, where the bloc became engaged after the criminal invasion and war initiated and led by the United States in 2003. These are examples of the goals of the dissemination of US and NATO military bases and of this offensive organization's expansion.

In the expansionist strategy, extra-regional partners of the military block now also include Colombia, the country with the most US military bases in South America, only matched by Peru. Following the election of an extreme right-wing government in Brazil, Brazil's partnership with NATO is a possibility, as per the suggestion of a former US Ambassador to the country, as is the realization of an agreement with the United States for the use of the space launch base of Alcântara, in the state of Maranhão.

We have reaffirmed that US and NATO military bases are imperialisms' outposts. For us, the world powers' goals, especially the United States, is to plunder the peoples' resources and control strategic routes, as well as to intimidate nations and ensure governments are submissive to imperialism.

In the final declaration of the World Peace Council's Assembly, in 2016, we strengthened our commitment to the struggle against the planet's militarization as one of the main threats to humanity, with the dissemination of military bases and NATO's expansion as some of its main expressions, as well as the modernization of nuclear arsenals and rising military expenditures.

Again, we confidently celebrate the development of this effort to expand our common struggle. Acknowledging the diversity of perspectives in the many points in the global overview, it is clear our commitment is based on a common principle, that is to seek world peace, to vehemently oppose war and aggression against the peoples, to build a fairer world free from the threats and devastation that accompany the imperialist powers' offensive policies grouped in NATO and led by the United States. We are certain that, together, we can defeat this march of destruction and death and demand an end to the race for an accelerated militarization of international relations and of the planet. For unity, I wish that our deliberations in Dublin are successful in favor of the consolidation of a broad and engaged global coalition.

Thank you.

Alfred L. Marder
President, U.S. Peace Council
USA

Dear Brothers and Sisters,

Thank you for this opportunity to speak to you at this historic gathering, historic because we have come together in unity, in the struggle against US/NATO imperialist policies. We have put aside any differences between us that inhibits the common goal.

The billionaires, the most arrogant, avaricious, aggressive section of the US ruling class, have captured the government. They have initiated a drive to undo all the social gains for which the people have fought for many years. They have instituted a killing budget of 61% of the total national treasure, 717 billion dollars. This does not include a trillion dollars for modernizing the nuclear arsenal. They have unleashed an atmosphere of racial animosity and attacks on immigrants and the foreign born. This is necessary for the acceptance of policies that have created the largest military institution in the world. The US economy is a war economy, enriching the bloated death merchants.

The so-called Democratic opposition party, for the most part, went along with this policy. In the recent national elections, the issues of war and peace and foreign policy, were deliberately ignored, not debated, by both parties. Cities and states are struggling to provide social services to their people, while the infrastructures are crumbling. The two ruling parties have united on an aggressive military policy that threatens world peace. The previous Obama administration moved 60% of the US military arsenal to the

Pacific which the present Trump administration has endorsed.

The US is involved in fourteen wars. It has a military presence in 183 countries, of the 196 members of the United Nations, with over 250,000 troops at an annual cost of 258 billion dollars to guarantee its global military financial and political dominance. US battleships sail in all the waters of the globe, armed with nuclear weapons, prepared for immediate response. Millions of people, hungry, homeless and desperate, have been fleeing their countries as a result of US interventions and collaboration.

The US has withdrawn from two major anti-nuclear weapons treaties. It has withdrawn from an agreement with Iran and its allies on Iran, creating an inflammatory situation. It uses its economic dominance to impose sanctions on many countries, sanctions that affect the living conditions of the people.

Its presence is to prevent the struggle of the peoples of the world for national independence, sovereignty and the choice of their national destiny. It openly threatens military action against Venezuela, Cuba and Nicaragua. The US is deeply involved in supporting undemocratic regimes in South and Central America.

We, the peace movement in the United States, recognize our historic responsibility of international solidarity. We fully recognize that the main threat to world peace emanates from US imperialist policies. We fully understand the complicity of the leadership of countries that have chosen to be the junior partners.

We know we cannot stop these policies alone. We need a united global peace movement. This is the responsibility that history has placed before us. We have taken the first steps by coming here together. We must alert our people; abolish US/NATO foreign military bases for world peace.

Thank you.

Silvio Platero
President
Cuban Movement for Peace and Sovereignty
of the Peoples (MOVPAZ)

Dear Comrades and Friends, Fighting for Peace,

I bring a greeting of peace from the Cuban people, and their reiterated promise to continue fighting for a better world, without the threat of nuclear attacks, war and imperialist meddling.

The presence of this incredible number of people fighting for peace across the globe, on the eve of the International Conference Against US/ NATO Military Bases, is irrefutable proof that united and mobilized, we can successfully confront the growing global threat of US imperialists and their allies at NATO, who are now pursuing a new global - and cyber - reconquest. This new conservative and neo-liberal wave that enthrones itself on a global scale is the result of ultraconservative and neo-fascist groups rising to power in the US, who wish to promote and impose their politics of domination and servitude on everyone in the world.

In this aggressive imperial strategy, the renewed effort of modernization and diversification of foreign military bases constitutes an essential component. Through this we see how the presence of these bases multiplies across the continents, particularly Latin America and the Caribbean. Along with the increased presence of these bases and installations, we have seen the reactivation of the US Southern Command and the US Fourth Fleet, which represent the most direct foreign threat to the preservation of the region as a zone of peace, as it was proclaimed by all the heads of state and governments in Latin America and the Caribbean in January 2014. Thirty-three heads of state and prime ministers opted for peace, and the resolution of such issues at the regional level, without the attendance of either the US or Canada at that meeting.

Cuba has the unfortunate privilege of having within its borders, in a manner both illegal and contrary to the will of its people and government, the oldest US military base in the world (at 115 years), which is the Guantánamo Bay Naval Base. The return of this occupied land and installation, along with the lifting of the trade embargo — through which the United States of America has imposed its control over the Cuban people for more than fifty years – has been one of the chief demands of all the peace-loving people and governments of the world.

Specifically, the village of Guantánamo will host, from the 4th to the 6th of May of 2019, the VI International Seminar for Peace and the Abolition of Foreign Military Bases, where, like many times before, hundreds of people fighting for peace will gather together, uniting their voices, and demand: a) the closing of this base, which has since been twisted into an oppressive, international centre of torture and human rights violations against detainees of Muslim origin and b) the unconditional return of the territory on which this base is embedded to the Cuban people. It was in these summits [BAHMAN: I think he means seminars] that many global initiatives were launched for the people and against the military bases, and many of these initiatives are taking shape now. What is happening here tonight is everyone's wish, the Cuban people's and of all those fighting for peace in Latin America and the Caribbean, the World Peace Council (WPC), PANA and all of the peace organizations are here tonight to recognize a World Day for Peace and Against Foreign Military Bases. We have proposed the 23rd of February, which was the day that the rental agreement for the Guantánamo Bay Naval Base was signed between the United States of America and the puppet President governing Cuba at the time. The base is now one hundred and fifteen years old and no legal convention exists that realistically maintains it legally for the North American government. It is a vagary of that government, a way to demonstrate its arrogance and a refusal to accept having a small, revolutionary, independent island on its doorstep [Bahman: I would add in "on its doorstep] that will always be independent.

Moreover, this first international conference that is starting in Dublin and the proposed creation of a Global Coalition of Organizations against these imperialist installations, upheld and encouraged by the United States

Peace Council, PANA and the WPC, were first conceived and preliminarily debated at these seminars in Guantánamo. There are direct actors here like the President of the United States Peace Council, Alfred L. Marder, whom we saw in the previous video, whom we tried to have on for ages, but it was necessary first to create the proper conditions in order to achieve what we have done here tonight.

We are certain that, at the height of these initiatives and the creative application of actions to motivate our nations, we can redouble the claim for the dissolution of the military base at Guantánamo, and all of the other such bases around the world, and in so doing, strike decisively against the imperialists' resolve to impose their global domination.

Thank you very much.

Dr. John Lannon
Member of the National Executive
Peace and Neutrality Alliance
Ireland

Ireland claims to be a neutral state, but has hitched itself to not one, but two military powers.

We've signed up to the EU's Permanent Structured Cooperation on Security and Defence (PESCO). We're fully supportive of efforts to strengthen EU security and defence and cooperation with NATO, the European Defence Fund and the European Defence Industrial Development Programme. We're on track to become part of an EU army.

We also keep ourselves attached to US warmongering by providing a *de facto* military base on our west coast.

For many decades, Shannon Airport has been a transatlantic gateway between Europe and America. Since the 1940s it has also supported a thriving tourist industry in Ireland's mid-west region, and it spawned the world's first duty free industrial zone.

In 2002, the Irish Government took a decision to provide landing and refuelling facilities to the US military at the airport. This followed UN Security Council Resolution 1368, which requested states to work together to bring to justice those responsible for the September 11, 2001 attacks, and which the US used to claim legitimacy for its invasion of Afghanistan. Early in 2003, just four weeks after 100,000 people marched in Dublin to oppose Irish support for another US invasion, this time Iraq, the Dáil [the lower house of the Irish Parliament] supported the decision of the Government to maintain these arrangements for what became a protracted and bloody war.

Since then, close to three million US troops and their personal weapons have passed through Shannon Airport on the way to and from the Middle East on flights that are officially classified as civilian. The numbers were at their highest in 2005 when 341,000 passed through, and dropped to just below 61,000 in 2017. The flights are governed by the Air Navigation (Carriage of Munitions of War, Weapons and Dangerous Goods) Order 1973, which prohibits the carrying of "munitions of war" through Irish airports or airspace, except where the Minister for Transport has given an exemption. In 2017 the Minister gave exemptions for 334 flights, with the personal weapons of troops on board, to land at Shannon. Permission was granted for a further 540 flights to take weapons through Irish airspace.

Aircraft operated directly by the US Air Force and Navy have also landed at Shannon. These include C-130 Hercules turboprops capable of carrying cargo or passengers, Boeing KC-135 Stratotankers used for aerial refuelling, and US Air Force and Navy executive jets. Despite Irish Government claims that these are not carrying arms, ammunition or explosives and are not involved in military operations or exercises they get special protection by the Irish authorities.

Any foreign military aircraft landing at an Irish airport or passing through Irish airspace must have permission from the Minister for Foreign Affairs to do so. In 2017 there were 515 requests for landings at Irish airports. The majority (402) were for US military aircraft landing at Shannon.

Successive Irish governments have claimed that the US military use of Shannon Airport is consistent with Ireland's policy of military neutrality. The concept does not exist in international law but nonetheless has been used by Ireland to denote non-membership of military alliances. However, the practice as currently implemented is not consistent with the responsibilities of a neutral country under the Hague Convention of 1907 on the Laws and Customs of War on Land. The Convention states that "belligerents are forbidden to move troops or convoys of either munitions of war or supplies across the territory of a neutral power." And even though Ireland hasn't ratified the Hague Convention, a 2003 High Court judgment in Horgan v An Taoiseach [Prime Minister] *et al.* stated that the State was in breach by allowing US troops to use Shannon on their way to and from war in Iraq.

Shannon Airport has also been identified as a stopover point in the US Government's extraordinary rendition programme. Between 2002 and 2008 individuals suspected of terrorism were secretly apprehended and transferred to CIA-run prisons or "black sites". The unlawful renditions were conducted with the facilitation and participation of foreign states that detained individuals and prepared them for transfer, or allowed their airports and airspace to be used for rendition flights. The CIA used front companies like Aero Contractors to transport detainees via private aircraft. Two known Aero rendition planes with registrations N379P and N313P were both recorded at Shannon Airport on numerous occasions. As a case in point, N379P landed there on 22 July 2002 on its return journey to the US after taking UK resident Binyam Mohammed to Morocco where he was tortured. Binyam was subsequently detained without charges in Guantanamo Bay between 2004 and 2009.

According to the Council of Europe and the European Parliament, the Irish Government is one of the states avoiding its international human rights responsibilities by refusing to investigate allegations that aircraft linked to renditions have landed at Shannon or have been permitted to cross Irish airspace.

There has been protest and non-violent action against the US military use of Shannon since it started in 2002. There were a number of high profile court cases, and acquittals. There are currently four peace activists going through the courts. And we have regular monthly peace vigils at the airport. Our colleagues in the Peace and Neutrality Alliance (PANA) host a similar monthly vigil outside the Irish Foreign Ministry in Dublin.

Sometimes it feels like the US military operation of the airport isn't real — it's only happening in another parallel universe. Go to the Shannon Airport website, you'll see nothing about it. Look at their reports and statistics of landings – no mention. From the mainstream media, not a whisper. But as activists we have learned to be persistent. Standing outside the airport on a cold December afternoon highlighting complicity in the mass murder of war is not what those of us who gather would like to be doing. But we do it.

One of the reasons it is worthwhile is because we could get rid of the US military from Shannon. They offered to leave once, and the Irish government of the time said, no, stay. But governments can change. And some day in the future an Irish Government may even listen to public opinion.

A 2016 Red C poll indicated that 55% of Irish adults believe the US military should not be allowed to use Shannon Airport. Yet, sixteen years after it became a cog in the never ending "war on terror'", it is, as I have said, a *de facto* US military base in a country whose leaders cling to their increasingly untenable claim of neutrality.

The maintenance of peace and security is a goal of Ireland's foreign policy. So is the protection of human rights. All we are trying to do is to achieve those goals.

Hiroji Yamashiro
Director, Okinawa Peace Action Center
Japan

I'm Hiroji Yamashiro, Chairman of the Okinawa Peace Action Center.

Okinawa is in the southernmost area of Japan and consists of many islands. It was the site of the bloodiest, most decisive battle for the Japanese and the US military at the last stage of World War II, with heavy civilian casualties.

During the US military occupation of Okinawa, they built huge bases and have never left.

The main island of Okinawa is overwhelmed by major military facilities, such as the US Air Force Kadena Air Base, which is called "the largest base in the Far East;" ammunition storage areas; Marine Corps Air Station Futenma and huge live-fire shooting ranges.

Citing the deterioration of the Futenma Air Station facility, US forces announced plans to build a new air field, despite fierce opposition from the people of Okinawa.

Takeshi Onaga, the former Governor of Okinawa, stood up against the new base plan, but became seriously ill in the midst of a tough dispute with the central government which is aggressively pushing the plan ahead. Unfortunately, he succumbed to his illness in August.

The people of Okinawa are grief-stricken by the loss of their truly great political leader, who was never afraid of speaking up against the central government. At the same time, they are outraged that the government chooses to follow the US rather than respecting the Okinawans' decision.

Overcoming the loss, however, the people in Okinawa elected a new governor, who inherited Mr. Onaga's will, defeating the opponent backed by the central government.

It is fully expected that the Japanese government will intensify oppression against Okinawa more than ever with a new governor who will never compromise with them.

I can imagine that the Japanese government won't listen to the request of the new governor at all. And against the sit-in protesters at the gate of USMC Camp Schwab, the government could send hundreds of riot police to remove them. We might see a lot of them injured or arrested.

I am so honored to be invited from Okinawa, which is under extreme pressure, and to be given a chance to speak at this global conference, where friends from all over the world gather with the intention of opposing the global presence of US military bases and wars waged by the US and its NATO allies, establishing a global coalition calling for international unity.

I express my sincere appreciation to the people who made our visit possible.

Two years ago, in October 2016, I was arrested during a nonviolent protest action, and was detained for a full five months. The district court found me guilty and gave me a sentence of two years in prison with hard labor with three years' suspended sentence.

Currently we are continuing to fight in the appeals court to overturn this decision, claiming that we are not guilty. Hiroshi Inaba, who is visiting Dublin with me, is my co-defendant and a trustworthy comrade.

We thank you very much for the warm support extended to us during our detention and our legal fight after our release. The support from the US and all around the world encouraged and empowered us a lot. I am so fortunate to have a chance to express our appreciation directly. Thank you so very much.

We face extraordinary difficulties and challenges in our movement to oppose the expansion of the bases of the US military along with the Self-Defense Forces of Japan schemes for potential war. However, we are determined to keep fighting in solidarity with you and to keep strengthening our connections.

Thank you again for making my participation possible and giving me this opportunity to report from Okinawa.

Let us strive together to create a peaceful world without military bases and war.

Thank you very much.

Moara Crivelente
Executive Director
Brazilian Center for Solidarity with the Peoples and
Struggles for Peace (CEBRAPAZ)
Brazil

Dear Friends and Fellows in our common struggle against US and NATO military bases,

It is a great honor to represent the Brazilian Center for Solidarity with the Peoples and Struggle for Peace (CEBRAPAZ) on this occasion. I wish to express our deepest appreciation to all organizers and to the Peace and Neutrality Alliance (PANA) for hosting us.

As members of the World Peace Council, we have been promoting and/or participating in various regional and global campaigns, and now in this broader, global initiative. These are essential steps in taking our struggle forward, making it more and more encompassing and effective.

US and NATO military bases are threatening peoples all over the world, as part of the logic of "deterrence" so cynically promoted by the main imperialist powers as components of their defense and security policies. NATO member states, especially the US and its closest allies, are themselves helping put humankind and the world at the brink of a disaster, by militarizing the planet and international relations *per se*, and, on another scale, feeding on tensions and insecurity in various countries, aiming to replace governments and assure that more subservient regimes are put in place by sponsoring the most reactionary and conservative elites in those countries.

In a period of systemic economic crisis, since 2001 through 2019, the

United States will have spent almost $6 trillion in its wars in Afghanistan, Iraq, Syria and Pakistan, according to estimates recently presented in a study at Brown University, USA. Around half of those killed in those wars were civilians; millions were forced to flee their homes and seek refuge in other countries. But how many billions were spent and what damage was inflicted in other unconventional wars, aggression and operations of interference of all sorts, such as the kinds of "regime change" that so many regions like Latin America have experienced, have yet to be estimated.

Most of the eighty US military bases and other such facilities in Latin America and the Caribbean are concentrated in Colombia and Peru, which border Venezuela and Brazil. Many of these and other bases are or can be used by NATO, such as the UK's base in the Malvinas Islands, usurped from the Argentineans. The US also counts on its Fourth Fleet and its Southern Command to keep the region under its radar and its threats.

However, some in NATO say the bloc does not need a massive military presence in Latin America because the US has good partners in the region and can always count on the Organization of American States (which the Cuban diplomat Raúl Roa García famously called the US "Ministry of Colonies"). But these institutions are intertwined. A recent example was the OAS Secretary-General's indication, following Trump's lead, that Venezuela could go through a military intervention or an internal military coup to remove President Nicolas Maduro from Government.

Argentina's President, Mauricio Macri, offered the US the chance of implanting more military bases in that country and Colombia took their special role in the US geostrategic view a huge step forward by becoming a NATO "global partner," the first in the region.

After the coup d'état that overthrew President Dilma Rousseff in Brazil, in 2016, the new, illegitimate government quickly restored the deals that had been dismissed, especially that of the surrender of Brazil's sovereignty over the Alcantara Launch Base, which the US demanded be put under its purview. In an environment of extreme antagonism inflated by a heavy media campaign, the putschist forces in the judiciary threw Lula in jail — fearing he could win this year's Presidential elections — and a neofascist character, Jair Bolsonaro, was elected President while openly pledging his serfdom to the United States and Israel. He announced outrageous appointments that include, as Brazil's Foreign Minister, a conservative diplomat known for campaigning for him and, worst of all, praising Donald Trump as "the West's savior." The next Brazilian President's position will be an international stance totally contrary to that promoted by Lula and Dilma's governments, which sought to contribute to the most important debates, foster multilateral institutions and defend the principle of sovereignty while struggling for a world of cooperation, globally and regionally. Examples are organizations such as UNASUR and CELAC (the Community of Latin-American and Caribbean States), which not long ago, in 2014, declared the region a Zone of Peace.

These are some of the challenges contextualizing our region and our struggle against its militarization. In Latin America and the Caribbean, in Brazil and in CEBRAPAZ, we strengthen our commitment with our common struggle for a fairer world, against wars, aggression and interventions, oppression, exploitation and all sorts of interferences that violate nations' sovereignty in favor of the imperialist powers' agendas, causing such suffering and preventing the peoples from charting their course independently. The US and NATO military bases are clear, material and threatening expressions of these powers' policies of fear, control and domination to which the peace-loving forces will not submit. Together we know we can face these threats and make the peoples' voices for a world of a just peace sound louder.

Dr. Stelios Socofli
President, Cyprus Peace Council

Dear Friends, dear Comrades,

First of all I would like to thank you for your most kind invitation to participate in this timely discussion against NATO-USA military bases hosted by the Peace and Neutrality Alliance (PANA). I would like to express my special thanks to the peace movements of the USA and Ireland.

At the same time, I would like to convey the best wishes of the Cyprus Peace Council for a fruitful exchange of views regarding the current state of play in a world which is bogged down in a serious, if not unprecedented, crisis. The increase in exploitation, oppression and conflicts is immense.

Despite efforts to silence what is happening all over the globe and numb the conscience of the people, the truth is blunt: our world today faces the threat of huge catastrophes, the disastrous consequences of which are impossible to limit to the national borders of the war zones and of the countries suffering from extreme poverty and disease. Additionally, despite the demagoguery of the capitalist leaderships, they consciously attempt in the name of manufactured threats to turn back the social and national emancipation of the last century; to control the masses and defeat any voice or action of resistance to their aggressive policies.

This is equally true of the country that I come from. Despite the mere fact that Cyprus is geographically close to the Middle East, where everyday people die and suffer from war, hunger and disease, where people are constantly made refugees, where children are deprived even of their last belonging that is hope, our government insistently manipulates public opinion. Syria and Palestine are not an issue for them. On the contrary, whilst we strive to explain to the people what is actually happening in our war-torn region and that nobody is left unaffected by the disaster that is taking place, whilst we make every effort to explain what are the roots and causes of foreign interventions, of the arms race and the aggression against neighbouring sovereign states, of the brutal attack and murdering of innocent people, our government signs security agreements with the Israeli government, purports to find channels of cooperation with NATO, and most recently pretends not to have known of the presence and functioning of US military helicopters and aircraft in the areas of the so-called sovereign British bases in Cyprus.

Against this background, we remain committed to defying militarism, starting from our country and through supporting the common struggles of the World Peace Council. We thus remain committed to fight against the expansion of militarism in all its forms, to counter NATO's effort for global dominance which is facilitated by the EU, to stand against the militarist policies of the EU (including the alleged creation of an EU army) and, of course, for the termination of the presence and expansion of foreign military bases.

The role of the Cyprus Peace Council, has always been to defend the will of the progressive non-nationalist people of Cyprus, in both Communities, Turkish and Greek Cypriots, for self-determination and for an independent and demilitarized Cyprus. Unfortunately, the London-Zurich Agreements, which gave the Republic its independence, compromised both the sovereignty and the territorial integrity of Cyprus.

Despite the granting of independence, Britain, Turkey and Greece were made 'guarantor powers', whilst Britain secured for itself a strong military presence on the island through the establishment of military bases occupying a significant percentage of the territory of Cyprus. Hence, when we speak of the need for the demilitarization of Cyprus this must provide not only for the withdrawal of the Turkish troops but also for the removal of the British bases.

The reaction of the left progressive movement in Cyprus to the establishment of the British military bases in our country through the Zurich-London agreements was put into effect immediately; their legal status is disputed and their presence as such compromises our vision of the world as a community of peaceful coexistence and cooperation. We cannot ignore their use either in aggressive military operations in the region or in illegal espionage activities. And I would like to repeat what I said at the beginning:

recent publications reveal that contrary to the provisions of their establishment they are used by non-Commonwealth countries, the USA to be more precise. Furthermore, they have been used against Iraq, totally illegal expeditions. Their illegal use, added to their illegal presence, intimidates our people and certainly protracts the insecurity by which we anyway feel very much threatened, due to the illegal Turkish military occupation. Not to mention the unacceptable consequences of their presence to the ecosystem of the region and the claimed medical handicaps caused by the military establishments and activities in the British bases to the residents of surrounding areas.

From what I have mentioned, it becomes clear, I think, that for as long as the military bases are not removed, Cyprus' total independence will be repressed through the continuous presence of an anachronistic British colonial regime. And the wider region will remain under the constant threat of a proxy hub for espionage and aggressive operations. Having said that, significant as our struggle against the removal of the British bases from Cyprus is, the first priority for the demilitarization of our country remains the termination of the illegal Turkish military presence in Cyprus, the termination of the illegal occupation by Turkey of 37% of the territory of the Republic of Cyprus.

Your solidarity in our struggle to end the occupation is appreciated. We acknowledge and appreciate deeply your enduring support, even more so today. I won't repeat what might sound as a cliché, that we are now at a crucial juncture. But I shall stress that the next few months will prove critical as to whether the occupation will end and the people of Cyprus — Greek Cypriots and Turkish Cypriots — will be allowed to prosper jointly in a reunited homeland, without foreign interference, in conditions of peace. It is our firm belief that for this to happen, we must remain committed to the strategic goal of Bicommunal, Bizonal Federation; the agreed solution on the basis of which we have managed to achieve many significant convergences after years of negotiations.

Unfortunately, in the months following the stalemate of the Crans Montana talks, Switzerland, July 2017, we witnessed severe regression in the public rhetoric and the willingness of the leaderships of the two communities in Cyprus to re-engaging in the negotiations process in a meaningful manner. The rhetorical question which is presented to us is whether we, Greek Cypriots and Turkish Cypriots, can afford the perpetuation of the occupation, the embedding of the *status quo* and the *de facto* permanent partition of our country. We can't. On the contrary, we consciously resist and stand against the legalization of the 1974 twin crime that is equally being facilitated (a) by those who oppose the Bicommunal, Bizonal Federation and (b) those who support confederalist ideas with the aim of keeping the Greek Cypriots and Turkish Cypriots apart.

After all, it is our duty to struggle first and foremost against the local powers, which serve the politics of nationalism and chauvinism, against those who are willing under the pretext of insecurity to militarize our country further. And the best, the most concrete response to that is a comprehensive solution of the Cyprus problem, on an agreed basis, which is the only means for terminating the military presence of Turkey and generating opportunities for a truthfully progressive and promising future; and to set Cyprus' example for peace and demilitarization, through which social emancipation will become more feasible.

Fulvio Grimaldi
Independent Journalist
Italy

Friends, Comrades,

A greeting to all and wishes for success of this strategically important conference. A special greeting to my republican friends in the conference, given that I shared a part of their glorious struggle against British colonialism in the Six Counties, both as a reporter and photographer, and as a militant against colonialism and repression. I was with you before, during and after Bloody Sunday in Derry and, happily, my work and evidence given to the various enquiries on Bloody Sunday, provided a little contribution to the establishment of truth.

What I notice from various reports and speeches I listened to or read, is that the issue of Italy and the US and NATO military presence there is incredibly underestimated. Geography itself informs us of the geopolitically strategic position of my country *vis-a-vis* imperialist operations in the region and beyond. Since entering NATO, Italy has been covered with some ninety US and NATO military bases, among which are the strategic commands of US forces in the Mediterranean, Near Asia, the Middle East and Africa.

The NATO, US and EU aggression of Yugoslavia, between 1990 and 1999, which split this sovereign country into small, inoffensive parts, was militarily conducted from Italy, from where NATO forces occupied the Kosovo province of Serbia. Almost eighty days of uninterrupted bombings of Serbia were made possible by US and NATO air-raids taking off from Aviano base in north east Italy.

In two Italian bases, Aviano and Ghedi, the US hosts some ninety nuclear bombs, despite the fact that the Italian people voted in a referendum against any nuclear presence, civilian or military, on its soil. In Camp Darby, near the Mediterranean port of Livorno, the US has been running, since the fifties of the past century, its largest deposit of armaments in all Europe, capable of supplying with all kinds of weaponry US and NATO forces in the Mediterranean, Middle Eastern and African regions. Smaller US and NATO bases line the Italian coastline from north to south.

Gaeta, near Naples, hosts the US Sixth Fleet, whose nuclear submarines, once based in Sardinia, now have their port in Augusta, Sicily, while the headquarters of the US Strategic Command of Central Region and all naval forces in Europe and Africa is in Naples.

Further south, in Sicily, the US runs two strategically decisive posts. Sigonella is the continent's most important drone base and was the starting point for most air raids carried out against Libya during the 2011 war, next to those taking off from US aircraft carriers. Not far from Sigonella lies Niscemi, where in recent years the US established their MUOS (Mobile User Objective System). This is the Italian element of a four-satellite stations complex, spread over the US, Europe and Australia, which runs the communications for all US military operations across the Globe.

It might be of interest, talking of bases that permit wars and aggression of various kinds, to know that since the end of World War II, in Capo Marangiu Base, Sardinia, the US trained and armed a huge contingent of Italian guerrilla forces and commandos. This force, which spread all over Italy, remained secret and totally illegal up to 1990, known only to Italian Intelligence and to some leading government figures. Its declared task was to "Stay Behind" (its official denomination) in the case of a Soviet invasion from the East. In reality, it was created to carry out disturbances and civil, war, in case the Communist Party won the election and thus entered government.

More could be added, but I will stop here as I am told that my time has run out.

It has become evident that the US and NATO apparatus in Italy is strategically the most important of all imperialist enterprises relating to the Balkans, Africa, the Middle East and Near Asia. It has been crucial for US, British, French and Italian operations that have lead to the obliteration of the Yugoslavian Federation, the destruction of Libya, the eight year long aggression in Syria and interventions in Africa starting with Somalia.

And let me add that I find it disconcerting that, so far, none of the delegations present has expressed any solidarity with the peoples of the nations attacked by the US and NATO. I consider it of the utmost urgency and political relevance to express the international anti-bases' and anti-imperialist movement's rejection of all US and NATO wars on innocent peoples and governments the capitalist West dislikes. I don't think the Movement will be up to its expectations and objectives unless it expresses its unconditional solidarity with those peoples and those governments, independently and against the imperialist propaganda efforts that systematically criminalize anybody who doesn't submit to neoliberal and globalist dictates issued from Washington, London, Paris and Berlin.

Lucas Wirl
Stoppe Base Ramstein
Germany

I would like to extend greetings from Kristine Karch to the organizers and to you all. She asked me this morning to substitute for her because she is sick and could not come to Dublin. In East and West Germany we had lots of military bases. With the end of Cold War, the fall of the Berlin Wall and the reunification of Germany, we got rid of all military bases except the US bases. This got me thinking. In Germany we still have many US military bases and they play an important strategic role for the USA. I would like to give you information on Air Base Ramstein. It is located south of Cologne and west of Frankfurt in a highly militarized area. There are many military bases located there, by the USA but also German military bases. Among others, the German Air Base Büchel, which holds about twenty US nuclear weapons stationed in Germany *via* NATO's nuclear sharing.

A commander of Air Base Ramstein stated the following: Air Base Ramstein is the largest, the most trafficked, best and one of the most important if not the most important military base in the world. Why did the commander make this statement? Air Base Ramstein is central to the US European Command. It is the headquarters of the Allied Air Command of NATO, including the nuclear command. It is the command center for missile defense. Thus you have the command of the sword and shield of NATO forces at Air Base Ramstein. It is also the headquarters of the US Air Force in Europe and Africa. And, there is a satellite relay station crucial for drone warfare. The former drone pilot, Brandon Bryant, informed the public on the role of Air Base Ramstein for drone warfare: Due to the shape of the

Earth no direct communication between a drone pilot in the USA and a drone in Yemen, Afghanistan or any other place in the region is possible. Air Base Ramstein is connected to the US drone pilot *via* cable, and the satellite relay station transports the signal to the drone. Without the satellite relay station no drone warfare.

I grew up in the nineteen eighties and nineties and witnessed the wind of change leading to the end of the Cold War era; the Warsaw Genuflection by Chancellor Brandt, President Richard von Weizsäcker speaking for the first time about liberation and not defeat that marked the end of World War II and the presence and importance of the slogan and statement "no more war no more fascism" for a reunified Germany. Having these themes in my mind it is hard to understand that the German government accepts the role of Air Base Ramstein and is not doing anything about it. There exists a status of forces agreement and it is possible for the German government to cancel this agreement.

In Germany, the Campaign Stop Air Base Ramstein was started in 2014. The campaign protests against drone warfare, demanding the immediate closure of the satellite relay station. The campaign also demands that the German government cancel the status of forces agreement and shut down Air Base Ramstein. The protests in 2019 will take place from June 20-30 with a peace camp, a blockade and other non-violent actions, a demonstration, cultural events and, for the third time, an international conference on no bases. I invite you to participate in the actions and would like to see us continue the discussions of this weekend in Ramstein.

Lastly I would like to give you information about the next NATO summit taking place on April 4th in Washington DC. NATO will celebrate its 70th anniversary. I would like to ask all of you to discuss with your groups at home how to participate in the protests against NATO around the summit. I do not want to repeat the analysis mentioned today but I would like to highlight the fact that NATO is the main driver for militarization on this planet. It is the largest weapons distributor in the world. It has global reach and focus with more than 100 partner countries. We need to overcome it. I agree with Mairead Maguire. We need a culture of peace but it is not possible with NATO. I hope there will be large united protests against NATO in Washington DC. We need to stand together in order to succeed.

Thank you very much.

Grigoris Anagnostou
President
Greek Committee for International
Détente and Peace (EEDYE)
Greece

Dear Fellow Fighters,

On behalf of the Secretariat of the Greek Committee for International Detente and Peace, I would like to express our greetings to all the participants present here.

I would like also to salute the initiative for the realisation of this international conference against US and NATO bases all over the world, especially in a period when the clouds of the war are becoming denser. Hotspots of war exist throughout the length and breadth of the planet, bringing to the fore the possibility of more local, regional and even generalised war. This is clear from the enormous concentration of private power in a number of combustible regions of the planet, especially in the Balkans and the southeastern Mediterranean.

In the light of these developments, the Greek Committee for International Détente and Peace took the initiative to publish a brochure that underlines the role of NATO and the EU as tools of capital against the peoples. This is an effort by our side to enlighten the people, to contribute to the discussion for revealing the criminal character of NATO and the EU against the peoples and to mobilise workers, the self-employed, women and youth against these organisations.

Dear Fellow Fighters,

The signature of Greek governments can be found under all NATO and EU summit meeting decisions. It is not at all accidental that recently the US Ambassador to Greece described our country and its Government as a "geopolitical hinge" and its government as a "preferred ally," expressing in this way the magnitude of the Greek government's involvement in imperialist planning.

That is why, amongst others, we underline that the SYRIZA-ANEL Government, supported by all the other bourgeois parties, bears a grave responsibility for the deepening involvement of our country in imperialist plans and wars. As of today, there exists about fifteen US and NATO installations in Greece, and our country spends 2.4% of its GDP per year — over €4.3 billion — on the needs of NATO.

In the name of "multidimensional foreign policy" and the "geostrategic upgrade" in order to attract investment, but also to export Greek capital to the border region of the Balkans, the Government has undertaken an active role on behalf of the US-NATO-EU, thus placing our people in great danger.

It has expanded and extended common interstate military exercises and co-training, within the framework of NATO, with the possibility of using, whenever necessary, both military and civil infrastructures (ports, harbours, highways, etc.), for the needs of imperialist organisation.

The extension of the Mutual Defense Corporation Agreement between Greece and the USA, which was signed in October of 2017 by the SYRIZA-ANEL Government, paved the way for Greece to become an enormous US-NATO base. Not only has the Government upgraded all existing bases and headquarters, such as the group of facilities in Crete (including the airbase, the naval base and the firing range), which play a special role in all imperialist interventions, but it has also created new facilities all over Greece. It is also discussing the possibility of transferring nuclear weapons to Araxos base.

In the light of these developments, the EEDYE has developed a miltitasked and consistent action with hundreds of mass mobilisations all over Greece, and especially in the regions that are host to NATO bases and headquarters. We have strongly and consistently opposed the anti-people policy of the government and the other bourgeois parties that promote the even deeper incorporation of our country into imperialist organisations. We have demanded our country's disengagement from NATO and the EU. This action provided a decisive response to the propaganda campaign that aims to dull people's awareness of any anti-NATO, anti-US, anti-imperialist expression, by hitting fascist and racist views and practices.

We note that the systematic condemnation of the criminal role of NATO, as the armed hand of Euro-Atlantic imperialism, must be combined with the revelation and condemnation of the role of EU and of the Common Policy of Security and Defense. The imperialist interstate Union (EU) and its tools are enemies of the peoples and the arguments that present the EU as a force for peace are groundless.

Dear Fellow Fighters,

We will continue strongly and decisively. We intend to step up our struggle with confidence in the inexhaustible popular forces. We believe that power should be in the hands of the people of the NATO countries to end this barbarity as a whole and once and for all. The peoples have never been, and never will be, alone when they they react and emerge on the scene. They hold a powerful weapon in their hands, which is their solidarity.

Opening Session

Keynote Speech

Chair: Ajamu Baraka
Black Alliance for Peace
USA

Chair's Opening Remarks

Ajamu Baraka
National Coordinator, Black Alliance for Peace
USA

Thank you, Bahman, for your leadership in pulling this important gathering together. It is indeed a pleasure and an honor to be with you this morning. It is a pleasure to see so many smiling faces this morning. This is a very, very important, and very critical, gathering here in this country at this particular moment in time.

I am glad to see so many of my friends and comrades from the US who are here this morning, particularly because many of you may not know that for us it is the middle of the night back in the US. But, in a way, that being the case it is like a metaphor for what we have to do to get ourselves prepared for the morning light — what we do here will determine what kind of day we will see at this conference and in this world.

So, I am happy to be here this morning, but I wanted to, before we got into the day, I wanted to thank everyone for their hard work in pulling this together. We know that PANA was absolutely critical and was able to secure this fantastic space.

Before we go further, I would like those individuals from the organizing committee who are here to stand so we could acknowledge and thank them also.

[Committee members stand – applause from audience.]

It is more than a notion to pull these kinds of gatherings together. It is a collective process and we see today the consequence of it.

Well my friends we are here this morning to start this day. We heard last night what was in fact a call to conference. The various voices from different experiences that shared with us the importance of this historic moment. The importance of the challenge we have before us — to build a movement, an international movement that would make it absolutely clear that we stand with the people of the world in opposition to the madness that we see.

This madness that says that war and aggression is inevitable, that says collective humanity must live with the scourge of war.

And at this moment when we see that this position has been normalized and reflected in this madness that we saw coming out of Europe in the last week or so around the discussion of the creation of a European army. The fact that that proposal did not meet with the level of rejection and disgust that one would normally expect that a proposal like that would meet reflects that task we have before us this weekend.

Our task is to confront and defeat this normalization of war. This acceptance that war and aggression is inevitable. And we are going to meet that challenge, this gathering this weekend is the gathering that will prepare us for that fight.

We are not only looking at the activities of empire, the US Empire and its obscene proliferation in the form of US bases, but we have connected that to our concerns with NATO.

NATO being in essence, along with the US Empire, the militarized wing of this 500 plus year Western, colonial/capitalist European project. And we identify that military arm as in fact the enemy of peace.

And we do that because it is absolutely necessary for us to stand in solidarity with the populations of the planet who find themselves in the crosshairs of this military wing.

Those of us who live and reside in the west, the US and Western Europe in particular, have a responsibility to the people of the world to, in fact do, that.

That is our responsibility my friends.

So, I am not going to belabor much longer with my comments. I am here to basically moderate this session and to bring to you our very special guess.

We have with us this morning a very important friend to the movement, a comrade who has been part of this struggle for freedom and liberation on this planet for many, many years.

Dr. Aleida Guevara-March is the daughter of Che Guevara and Aleida March. She is a pediatrician at William Soler Children's hospital in Havana and teaches at the Escuela Latina-Americana de Medicina, Havana, and at a primary school for children with disabilities. She is the author of several scientific papers published in specialized magazines in Cuba and has presented at various conferences on issues of Public Health in Cuba and on other Cuban issues in Germany, Argentina, Brazil, Cyprus, Ecuador, Spain, France, Greece, India, Italy and Portugal, among other countries. She is the author of a book titled Chavez, Venezuela and the New Latin America.

Please join me in welcoming Aleida Guevara.

Keynote Speech

Dr. Aleida Guevara
Cuba

Good morning to you all.

As you may know, I speak Spanish.

For me it is a great privilege to be here with you and to meet and get to know in person men and women who have devoted most of their lives to the fight for the most beautiful cause, which is the fight for life. For me, it is really a great privilege to be here with you and to spend time with you all. There are so many things I would like to share with you. Sometimes the ideas go round and round in my head and are not very well organized but you know very well that I come from an island that unfortunately has borders. Islands normally should only have borders with the sea. That is why we are islands. The natural border would be the sea and that's it. However, there are many islands around the world that unfortunately have borders because they have been invaded; they have been damaged as people. In my case, in the case of my people, we have a border with a military base, a North American army base imposed against the will of the people by what amounted to a puppet government that allowed such a thing to happen. We still today suffer the presence of this military base on our national territory.

Since the Cuban revolution, we have fought in international fora to denounce the base at Guantánamo. The Cuban Government, which is the one representing the Cuban people, does not want the base there. This is different from other countries whose governments are happy to host military bases. This is not the case with Cuba. The Cuban Government does not want the base, which was imposed not just against the will of the people but also against the will of the Cuban Government. For many years we have spoken, argued, assessed the situation. The Cuban Government rejected all possibility of co-operation with the base — no water supply, no electricity supply. It costs the US millions of dollars to remain at Guantánamo. However, they have remained. Firstly, because Cuba is like a thorn in their hearts and they are trying to injure the dignity of the Cuban people, and they really hurt the Cuban people. From Guantánamo, mercenary attacks have been launched on fraternal people like the people of Santa Domingo and Puerto Rico. For Cubans, this is painful as these people are our brothers and sisters and the attacks have been launched from our national territory.

In the last few years, as everyone knows, the base has become a detention centre with no legal jurisdiction, where the people detained there are treated like animals. They are subject to torture and the Cuban people don't want this. We cannot do what we would really like to do, which is to get rid of this base in our land. We can't do it because it would give the US the perfect excuse it is waiting for to attack us. We are not afraid of them but Cuba needs peace to continue its development and in order to be useful to other brotherly people. We have only one way — diplomacy — to demonstrate to the world that this piece of land has been stolen from our people and must be given back to them. This is not what the US is waiting for. They want the Cuban people to take an initiative that would justify an invasion.

The objective of the base — in theory — is to defend US citizens in the region. In principle, that was the main reason for the base. But if we think clearly about this how many bases should Mexico have in the United States where there are twenty-four million Mexican citizens? If this was really the reason for the base it is absurd. Even worse, we know that many American parents send their children to these bases as a way of seeing the world but they don't know what their children are facing. What are their children going to become? The cold statistics: how many people have been attacked by US military personnel on these bases: women raped, children abused? Even worse, the way they abuse our land … with intoxicated reservoirs because US law does not allow material to be stored on their territory so what cannot be stored in the US is moved to our land. They don't care about that or that we have become collateral damage because unfortunately they feel superior. This is very negative for any people.

I had to live that experience myself personally. I suffered for my skin. I worked for a year as a physician in Nicaragua. I remember there were a group of doctors from the US training Nicaraguan doctors. It was embarrassing. They were nice people. They had good will but they didn't have a clue. The Nicaraguan doctors were ten times better than the US doctors but we were like natives to the American doctors – like Indians, half naked! We are Indians, natives, very proud of it. We have to learn from them how to resist, how to survive centuries of exploitation. They are still there. They are still standing up. We should learn many things from these people.

As I was saying, islands should normally only have one border – and that would be a border with the sea. However, we have many islands that are not like that. We are in one of those islands today with a border in its own land because another country has part of its land under occupation. We could talk about Cyprus a third of whose territory is occupied by Turkey but there are British army bases in the unoccupied part. Why are they there and until when are they going to be there?

Thousands upon thousands of military bases are spread all over the world. Some have very specific purposes, for instance to control the main treasury of mankind — water. Yet, we do not mobilize.

Let's do a simple exercise. How many people here are under thirty? Some! That is really good. We have some young people here. You are going to take the relay from us. We have to work with the young people as they are the guarantee that what we have been fighting for — the constant struggle by men and women all over the world — will not be lost.

We are facing a serious problem — a lack of information. There is a manipulation of information, constantly, and this is very damaging. The education that most people in this part of the world receive creates a divide from the rest of the world. The first thing we have to address, therefore, is awareness that one part of the world is not going to survive without the other. Let us take a very simple example: something that most Europeans eat. The potato. Where does it come from? It comes from South America. We satisfied their hunger in the 15th and 16th centuries.

People, unfortunately, have very poor memories. They forget that the people who came to South America from Europe were migrant people who migrated because they suffered from famine, wars, fears and desperation. That is what happened it is sad to say. No one is going to leave their country for pleasure. Most of the people who migrated were obliged to do so because they had no hope, they were hungry, they were poor and they were victims of war.

We have to bring back our historical memory. We must have more solidarity. We must learn to cherish what we have in order to share what we have with other people. We still need to grow a lot as human beings. It is very important to have the proper information.

Last night I was ashamed. How often have I been to Italy, to the Italian solidarity movement? Many times. I was not aware of the many NATO military bases in Italy. There is no reaction to them in Italy. I don't feel it. Why is that the case? We cannot say that Italians are asleep. Italians have a long history of struggle. That force is still there but it has to be awakened. We need to shake them, to touch them.

We do not do enough in these types of gatherings. This conference is the first step. It has to be multiplied. The information has to be spread among thousands and thousands of men and women. Only together will we be strong enough. This has been seen in a very small island in the Caribbean. We are still there, still standing with our socialist revolution only ninety miles from the most powerful economic and military force in the world. We are all united. Our people are all united. Our people are strong.

This strength we have to find together. We need it. We need to have information, to have unity. To have unity we need mutual respect. We need to have common goals. We need to leave behind the small differences between organizations. We need to have common goals for our fight. That is the way we have to work. What is our goal today? No more wars. No more military bases. We have to be united in our fight to achieve these goals.

We need to work together. We need to reach the human fibre. To do that, we need to be in contact with the people. A farmer — a peasant — doesn't understand a project that is very sophisticated. He understands his land and we must show him that military bases are poisoning the land so that they cannot grow crops. The peasant will join the fight.

These are just a few words. Sometimes we forget that we must claim them back to achieve unity. We badly need to keep on working. We have a long road in front of us but we are there. We are on the right path. We have devoted the best years of our lives to this work.

I had the privilege of serving in Nicaragua as a doctor and then I went to Angola. I lived there for two years and learned a lot during those two years. I learned to reject everything relating to racism. Human beings must not be judged by the colour of their skin but by their ability to help others. I reject everything to do with colonization. We cannot exploit others. We cannot impose our culture on others. We cannot attack the identity of other people. We haven't the right to do that and we must fight that. We must realize that we can. Yes, we've proven it.

The world does not need weapons. The world needs medicines. The world does not need weapons. The world needs food. The world does not need weapons. The world need solidarity, understanding, unity and strength to create the better world that we all need.

When I was very young, a young writer from Puerto Rico came to Cuba. Puerto Rico is still a colony of the United States. It is shameful what they have to suffer. Remember the last storm in the Caribbean. We experienced storm damage throughout most of our island but we restored our electricity supply in seventy-two hours. Puerto Rico was also affected by the storm but some people there are still suffering with no electricity. We would have liked to help them with all the love in the world — they are our brothers and sisters — but the United States would not allow us. What right have they to do that? These are the things that hit us hard.

That young Puerto Rican writer left a verse of one of his songs: "Go back home. Leave my country."

Plenary 1:

Militarism, Nuclear Weapons, and Military Bases

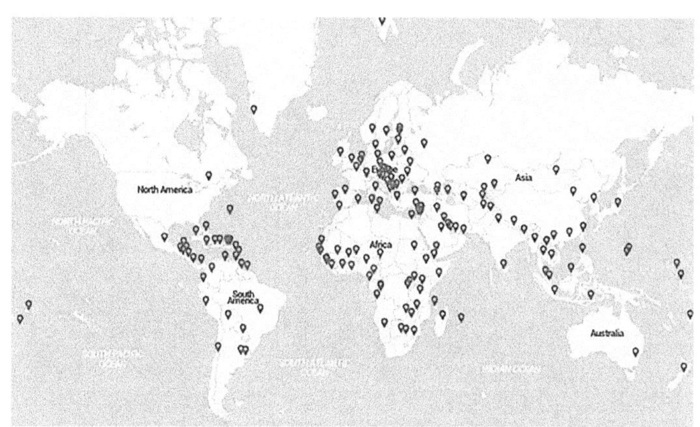

Chair: Dr. Margaret Flowers
Popular Resistance
USA

Chair's Opening Remarks

Dr. Margaret Flowers
Co-Director, Popular Resistance
USA

Before we start this session, I would like to make a few remarks to put our discussion in context. This panel is on militarism, nuclear weapons and military bases. The US is a fading empire and even the Pentagon has recognized this in the Post Primacy Report of 2017. A recent report from the Congress found that the US' new national security strategy, which is to be able to take on the Great Powers, Russia and China, is not something that the US has the capacity to realize. To quote the chairman of the committee that produced the report, Eric Edelman, he said, "US military superiority is no longer assured." A good thing? Right. And another report, the Annual Industrial Capabilities Report, found that the US does not have the industrial capacity to take on the Great Powers. The Pentagon's response is to ask for three things: more money, more weapons and more intelligence gathering capacity.

A recent audit of the Pentagon, which the Pentagon failed, found that it is a 2.7 trillion-dollar organization. This amounts to 62% of federal discretionary spending, leaving too little for other important areas of public policy such as energy, education, healthcare and housing. How much more can the US spend on the military while the infrastructure of the US continues to fade and the social security safety net continues to crumble? How much more can the US spend to try to hang on to the last vestiges of power while what the world needs most is cooperation?

Every year, tens of billions of dollars continue to be appropriated by the Congress for the Pentagon — sometimes more than the Pentagon asks for. This is not surprising as, in the US, we have two war parties. In the most recent mid-term elections, the group that won was war. More and more elected representatives are veterans of the military or the security state. There was a coordinated effort to persuade more military veterans to run for Congress on behalf of the war parties.

This is a dangerous time. The US is heading in a dangerous direction as the empire fades. The world recognizes this. The call for a European army to protect Europe from China, Russia and the United States is concerning. We are entering another accelerated arms race. The US has committed a trillion dollars towards our nuclear weapons program. The US is isolating itself as it imposes economic sanctions on other countries that are hurting the people in those countries and are causing other countries to work together to get around those sanctions.

Putting all this into context, we can see the importance of gatherings like this. There must be more international solidarity to help the world navigate through this dangerous time to avoid hurting too many people.

Our first speaker on this panel is Dr Dave Webb, Chairman of the Campaign for Nuclear Disarmament (CND) in the UK. Dave is Emeritus Professor of Engineering at Leeds Beckett University in England where he switched subjects and faculties to become Professor of Peace and Conflict Studies. He is now retired and focuses mainly on campaigning for peace."

Dr. Dave Webb
Chair
Campaign for Nuclear Disarmament
UK

Thank you very much for the introduction and thank you also to all the organisers and participants of this very important and timely conference. Now must be the time for us to come together to oppose militarism and the global power structures epitomised by foreign military bases.

This session focuses on bases associated with nuclear weapons and for the UK this has involved maintaining some of the overseas bases of its dwindling empire and hosting others from the growing (now struggling) US Empire.

During the Second World War the UK allowed the US free access to a number of Royal Air force (RAF) airfields and US forces have stayed in some of these ever since. Others have been increasingly employed in US military intelligence gathering operations and have ensured that the US-UK 'Special Relationship', where the US military is allowed to remain in occupation, continues to this day.

After the Second World War, the US Air Force (USAF) remained as part of the United States Air Forces in Europe (USAFE). The legal basis for the US Visiting Force in the UK is primarily the NATO Status of Forces Agreement (SOFA) of 1951 and the Visiting Forces Act of 1952. The SOFA allows US military forces to operate within, and at the consent of, the UK and the Visiting Forces Act incorporates the SOFA into UK law. Together, they provide the overarching framework for the stationing of US forces in the UK.

This has been something the Campaign for Nuclear Disarmament has been very concerned about for over 60 years. In the mid-1950s public concern over the Cold War and the build-up of nuclear weapons was growing rapidly. In May 1957 Britain exploded its first fusion bomb and later in November, the writer JB Priestley published an article in the *New Statesman* called "Britain and the Nuclear Bombs", which called for unilateral nuclear disarmament. There was a massive public response leading to the suggestion that there was a need for a mass movement against nuclear weapons.

Then, in December 1957, Britain agreed to receive US Thor intermediate range nuclear missiles. The US would provide the missiles, training and parts for five years of operation and the UK would provide the bases and supporting facilities. An understanding was reached in February 1958 about where to station them (at RAF Feltwell in Norfolk and RAF Hemswell in Lincolnshire) and a formal agreement followed in June. But February 1957 was also when the very first meeting of the Campaign for Nuclear Disramament (CND) was held in London, and was attended by 5,000 people. CND supported the first of the major Aldermaston Marches the following year, organised by the Direct Action Committee Against Nuclear War (DAC). Thousands joined the four-day march from London to the Atomic Weapons Establishment at Aldermaston, to demonstrate their opposition to nuclear weapons. Since then CND has focussed its campaign mainly on British nuclear weapons and the bases in the UK that the US has used to station its nuclear weapons and from which its military aircraft bomb and destroy countries such as Yugoslavia, Iraq, Afghanistan, Libya, Syria and threaten others — such as Russia and China.

In July 1958 the US and UK settled on a Mutual Defence Agreement and they have cooperated extensively on the development of nuclear weapons ever since. This has involved the exchange of scientific data and fissile materials. The UK closed its missile development programme in 1960 and instead purchased (as with Polaris) or leased (as with Trident) US missiles. These US missiles are then fitted with UK-US developed warheads as part of the UK's so-called 'independent nuclear deterrent.' The US also supplied the RAF and the British Army in Germany with nuclear weapons until 1992 and nuclear-capable USAF aircraft were based in the UK from 1949 until 2006 when they were finally withdrawn. However, in June 2017 it was reported that, amid growing tensions with Russia, the US had deployed its full range of strategic bombers to Britain for the first time in history. Two B-2 stealth bombers, three B-52H Stratofortress aircraft and three B-1B Lancers were exhibited at the Fairford Air Show. Apparently, the Pentagon considered it necessary to remind Moscow of America's strike capability.

During the Cold War, British nuclear warhead stockpiles grew to a maximum of 520 in the 1970s but since then the delivery systems and warheads have been gradually reduced. In 1998 the UK finally decommissioned its WE.177 bomb, leaving the Trident system, consisting of four Vanguard nuclear submarines based in Scotland, as the one and only nuclear delivery system. The reduction has occurred as a result of rising costs and technical problems but also because of public disapproval and protest.

During the late 1950s there were several accidents involving US nuclear weapons in the UK. At least two of these could have led to a nuclear explosion or even worse. In July 1956 a US bomber crashed into a storage igloo containing three Mark 6 nuclear bombs at RAF Lakenheath. The resulting fire damaged the bombs, but luckily did not ignite their conventional explosive triggers.

Then, in January 1958, a wheel casting of a B-47 failed during an exercise. It is not clear where the airbase was, but a likely candidate is Greenham Common Airbase. The aircraft carried one weapon in strike configuration and the tail struck the runway and a fuel tank ruptured. The aircraft caught fire and burned for seven hours. The high explosive contents did not detonate, but there was some contamination in the immediate area of the crash. The wreckage and the asphalt beneath it were removed and the runway washed down. There have been many accidents of this type involving nuclear weapons at US bases around the world.

Another accident occurred at Greenham Common in September 1959 when a US aircraft in trouble dropped two large fuel tanks shortly after take-off. One hit a parked aircraft nearby, which had a nuclear bomb on board. Two people were killed in the resulting fire which took sixteen hours to put out. The area around the base was radioactively contaminated. This incident was kept secret until details were uncovered by CND in 1996. Of course, we have no idea how many other nuclear near misses have taken place, although we are fairly sure that none resulted in a nuclear explosion.

Greenham Common is probably most famous for the protest that was organised by the women's movement that developed from the peace camps established from 1981 in protest at the deployment of US cruise missiles there. The women's 19-year protest, often involving blockades of the base and cutting through the fence, drew worldwide media and public attention. As a consequence of the protests there and across Europe, Reagan and Gorbachev eventually signed the Intermediate-Range Nuclear Forces Treaty

(INF) in 1987 that removed a whole range of US and Soviet short and intermediate range nuclear weapons from Europe. The same treaty that Trump is now threatening to withdraw from and to take us back thirty years. The US returned Greenham Common to the UK in September 1992 and in 1997 Greenham Common was made public parkland.

In 1980 Molesworth became the focus of protest when it was decided to house sixty-four US cruise missiles there. A peace camp was established in December 1981 and it became a link in a Europe-wide network of centres for non-violent direct action (NVDA) in opposition to US and NATO deployment of Pershing II and cruise missiles. Since the removal of cruise missiles, Molesworth has been developed as a Joint Intelligence Centre and in October 2016 it became clear that it was helping to identify targets for US drone strikes. Other US bases in the UK at Menwith Hill in Yorkshire and Croughton, near Oxford, have also been implicated in these actions. Over $200 million is being spent to enlarge Croughton into a major intelligence and communications centre for NATO and the US. Three other US bases at Mildenhall, Alconbury and Molesworth are due to close and their functions and personnel transferred to Croughton or to Lakenheath. Croughton is already known to link with the US base at Ramstein in Germany and to have a fibre optic communications link with Camp Lemonnier in Djibouti to co-ordinate drone strikes over Yemen.

CND continues to campaign and to protest strongly on these issues, in the streets, in Parliament and at US bases and UK nuclear installations. Particular targets for protest and blockades are Aldermaston and Burghfield in the south of England, where nuclear warheads are developed and built, and Faslane in Scotland where the Trident submarines are berthed. A dedicated 'Nukewatch' group also monitors, tracks and, when and where possible, blocks the nuclear convoys that travel up and down the country carrying nuclear warheads to and from Faslane for refurbishment in the south of England. Faslane Peace Camp near the main gate of the base has been occupied continuously for over twenty-five years. It was established on 12th June 1982 and has taken up various positions alongside the base although it is now well established with mains water and planning permission for twelve caravans and the local council has decided not to waste money on a large-scale eviction.

The anti-nuclear protest in Scotland has been particularly strong and has also been taken up by the campaign for Scottish Independence. Blockades and protests at the Faslane base are frequent, supported by the peace camp. Last September a major international demonstration was organised by Scottish CND and featured speeches by activists and campaigners from various countries — including the US.

Despite our focus on UK nuclear weapons, CND realises the importance of the international campaign to abolish nuclear weapons and we have worked with the US, Japanese and European peace movements. We also campaign against US missile defence systems as an integral part of a nuclear first strike strategy — the shield to prevent retaliation from the first strike sword. The UK is involved in this system through two bases in Yorkshire — Menwith Hill and Fylingdales. As well as being a huge NSA electronic spy base, Menwith Hill has also been designated as a down-link station for space-based components of US missile defence. Also, some eighty miles away the pyramid-shaped Phased Array Radar at Fylingdales provides early warning and tracking and targeting data for US missile defence interceptors. The US interceptor missiles and radar bases in Europe stationed close to the border with Russia are heightening tensions and must also be opposed. Similarly, the introduction of the Theatre High Altitude Area Defence (THAAD) missile defence system, in South Korea and Japan, are aimed at Russia and China and not North Korea as claimed.

We have also worked as part of the International Campaign to Abolish Nuclear Weapons (ICAN) to help establish the UN Treaty for the Prohibition of Nuclear Weapons. In particular, the campaign to remove US nuclear weapons stationed under the NATO nuclear sharing agreement in Europe is of growing importance. Trump's determination to pull out of the INF treaty and to spend $1 trillion or more on a new generation of 'usable' nuclear weapons, some of which will be stationed in Europe, means that it is vital that we work together to remove all nukes from Europe. The majority of people around the world want to rid it of nuclear weapons — we are told they are for our protection but how can something that threatens our existence make us more secure?

We live in extremely dangerous times – climate change and nuclear annihilation are huge challenges that can only be overcome by global cooperation on a scale never seen before. We must show the way and work together to build a unified global opposition to militarism that is too strong and too determined to resist.

Iraklis Tsavdaridis
Executive Secretary, World Peace Council (WPC)
Greece

Dear Friends and Fellow Fighters for a World of Peace and Social Justice,

I am conveying militant peace greetings from the World Peace Council (WPC) and also on behalf of the Greek Committee for International Détente and Peace (EEDYE). Many thanks to the host organisation Peace and Neutrality Alliance (PANA), for its hard work as well as to the Coalition Against U.S. Foreign Military Bases, which made this important conference possible. We are proud of having contributed to this project with our forces.

With Dublin and Ireland we could not have found a better place to hold this conference, taking into account the long standing sentiments of the Irish people for the struggle for its independence, its anti-imperialist and anti-colonial struggles but also the current firm and principled position of the peace movement in Ireland expressed through PANA, which is strongly fighting against the further militarization of the European Union, the EU Battle Groups and Permanent Structured Cooperation (PESCO) but also against NATO, which is the armed wing of imperialism worldwide. We particularly hail and support the struggle of PANA against the use of Shannon Airport by the US Air Force, with thousands of flights landing in a *de facto* US base in Ireland on their way to commit the imperialist crimes around the world. We salute the Irish peace fighters from Liberty Hall in Dublin.

Our conference takes place in crucial moments for humanity and for peace and stability in the world. The aggressiveness of imperialism is increasing almost everywhere in the world. The aggravation of the capitalist crisis in previous years has intensified imperialist aggressiveness against the peoples. In a world where 0.7 percent of the population owns 46 percent of the wealth of the planet and the poorest 70 percent of the population owns a mere 2.7 percent, the inequalities are widening. Almost three and a half billion people (half of the world's population) live in poverty; 821 million live in hunger and 758 million do not have access to clean drinking water. At the same time, according to Stockholm International Peace Research Institute (SIPRI), world military expenditures rose to $1.7 trillion in 2017, a 1.1 percent increase compared to 2016. The USA alone had spent $610 billion and NATO member states together more than $900 billion. A small percentage of the above would be enough to combat and eliminate hunger and curable diseases in Africa and elsewhere in the world.

The USA, NATO and the EU, in their drive for world domination, are the greatest threat to peace and the peoples of the world. They are responsible for the exponential increase in military expenditure, and the race for new, more sophisticated and destructive weapons, namely, nuclear weapons. The escalation of interference, threats, provocations and destabilization operations intensify the danger of unleashing an escalation of conflicts that would lead to great and unimaginable consequences for humanity, including the use of nuclear weapons — that can and must be prevented.

Foreign military bases in the world are a "useful" and necessary tool for imperialist plans, wars and aggression. They constitute an instrument of domination of the powerful states as we have witnessed for decades in all corners of the world. The fact that about 90% of the foreign military bases belong to the US and/or NATO speaks for itself and explains the title and theme of our conference here in Dublin. While we oppose, as the WPC, on principle all foreign military bases in the world, we cannot close our eyes to the reality and the tendencies, namely, the historically aggressive character of NATO, which has been expanding since 1991 to the East, to the South and to Asia and Latin America. Despite the severe competition between NATO states, the USA remains the leading force that is confronting its main competitors on economic and geopolitical levels, namely, Russia and China, with military encirclement, "missile defence shields" and troops along their borders.

Coming from Greece, a relative small country but with an important geo-strategic location, we underline the extremely negative developments of the last few years, where our country has been transformed into a huge US/NATO military base, with fifteen old and new military installations,

NATO and EU headquarters, bases for drones and helicopters, and even the possibility for "hosting" again US nuclear warheads on our soil, in addition to the famous Souda Air and Naval Base in Crete, from where military aggression has been carried out against the peoples of the Middle East for many years. At the same time, Greece spends 2.4% of GDP on the needs of NATO, thus occupying second place among the member states (after the US), which in practice does not serve our country's security and defense, but rather serves NATO's operational plans. Greece has readjusted the principles of the armed forces to serve imperialist planning. At the same time, not only has it signed on to the aggressive military readjustment of NATO military forces to surround Russia, but it participates operationally and has in fact allowed NATO, on the pretext of the migrant issue, to place forces in the Aegean Sea at the invitation of the Greek government. Greece has become a privileged partner for the USA, it has the best ever relations and cooperation with Israel and shares the values of "Euro-atlanticism" for which it has received the appreciation of the US and other imperialists. It constitutes a provocation to the sentiments of the vast majority of the Greek people, who know about the criminal role of the USA and NATO in Greece and Cyprus, to observe this increasing alignment with imperialist plans and, furthermore, when it comes from a self-proclaimed "left" government. The Greek Peace Committee and other people's movements of the country are organizing, all over the country, political events, mass protests and demonstrations in front of the US Embassy uncovering and denouncing the reactionary and dangerous plans and demanding the disengagement of Greece from the imperialist organisms and plans.

The powerful military presence of the US in the world is enhanced by its fleets, such as the 6th Fleet in the Mediterranean Sea, the 7th Fleet in the Pacific Ocean, the 4th Fleet in South America, the Black Sea Armada and others, along with the Command Structure of the US military forces in all corners of the world. The US is using "bilateral military agreements" with dozens of countries through which it is using air space, ports, and airports for its armed forces and joint military exercises with various countries.

NATO, the biggest war machinery in history, is heading towards it 70th anniversary next year. A history full of crimes against humanity. Just in the last twenty years this has been demonstrated by the military aggression of NATO in Yugoslavia, Afghanistan, Iraq, Libya, Syria and Yemen. NATO has never been anything else than an offensive military structure in the service of capital and the multinational corporations. NATO, the armed tool of imperialism, decided unanimously at its last summit in Brussels (July 2018) to build by 2020: thirty mechanized battalions, thirty air squadrons and thirty combat vessels ready to deploy within thirty days or less. NATO is modernizing and increasing its arsenal aiming for a nuclear first-strike capacity against its opponents. We demand and struggle for the dissolution of NATO while supporting the struggle of the peoples in each member state to disengage from it.

The WPC strongly opposes the further militarization of the European Union as an instrument for the interests of the big capital and monopolies, and denounces the plans through Permanent Structured Cooperation (PESCO), the Batlle Groups and the "European Interventions' Initiative" that constitute dangerous tools for foreign intervention and imperialist aggression in many parts of the world. We observe with deep concern the steps toward the implementation of the plans to build an EU Army alongside and under the doctrine of "Pool and Share" with NATO. The European Union, alone or with NATO, is acting against its peoples. Therefore it is imperative to condemn the criminal role of NATO, as the armed wing of European-Atlantic imperialism, in connection with the revelation and condemnation of the role of the EU and its Policy of Common Security and Defense (PCSD). This imperialist interstate Union and its tools are enemies of the peoples, and the views presenting the EU as a "force for peace" are groundless and harmful.

A crucial area of work for the WPC remain to be the struggle for the complete abolition of all nuclear weapons and the opposition to the testing of any nuclear armaments. As historical initiators of the "Stockholm Appeal" in 1953 with more than 400 million signatures collected from all over the world, we consider the appeal more than valid today. The WPC denounces the recent announcement made by Donald Trump about US withdrawal from the 1987 Intermediate-Range Nuclear Forces Treaty (INF), which bans ground-launched nuclear missiles with ranges from 500 to 5,500 kilometers. This constitutes a further escalation of imperialist aggression and of its plans for the militarization of outer space. The WPC supports the Treaty on the Prohibition of Nuclear Weapons as a step toward their total elimination but we have to state that we are not sitting on a sofa counting only the number of states while imperialist aggression is continuing by all means around the world.

Dear Friends,

Without underestimating any other region or hot-spot today, I would like to draw your attention to the situation in the Middle East. The area is known for its rich mineral resources and geo-strategic importance for powerful states. Imperialists have never hesitated, and do not hesitate, to use all kinds of mechanisms, including armed fundamentalist mercenaries from more than 80 countries (in the case of Syria), to bring countries and governments under their control. The defeat of ISIS in Syria and Iraq, despite its significance, does not mean the end of the crisis. Very recently the WPC carried out an International Solidarity Mission to Syria, in order to express our solidarity with the people of Syria, which has been through huge suffering and losses over the last seven years, due to imperialist interventions and military operations. Large number of troops, including from Turkey in the north, from the USA in the north east, and smaller contigents from various other NATO states, are still present in Syria, threatening the territorial integrity, sovereignty and unity of the country. We especially express our solidarity with, and our deep concern for, the suffering people of Yemen, who are under heavy attack from the Saudi-led coalition with the full support of the USA, a criminal act of aggression that we strongly condemn.

The core obstacle to peace in the Middle East continues to be the Palestinian issue. We strongly denounce and condemn the murderous actions of the Israeli regime and its army in Gaza and in the occupied West Bank, which, in the past few months, have resulted in hundreds of Palestinian victims, most of whom were brutally killed or injured during peaceful protests against Israel's actions and policies. The WPC strongly opposes and condemns the US administration's irresponsible and illegal decision to move its embassy from Tel Aviv to Jerusalem, a city with a clearly defined multi-ethnic and multi-religious character and status as specified in UN Resolution 181. The efforts for the judaization of Jerusalem and the Basic Law — "Israel the Nation-State of the Jewish People" — adopted by the Israeli Parliament — constitute an attempt to establish a *de jure* apartheid state with the oppression of all non-Jewish citizens.

The WPC reiterates its solidarity with the Palestinian people for their inalienable right to an independent State within the borders of pre-June 4th, 1967, with East Jerusalem as its capital. We demand an end to the occupation of Palestinian territory by the settlements on the West Bank and in Jerusalem, as well as of the Syrian Golan Heights and the Lebanese Shebaa farms. We further demand the release of all Palestinian prisoners from Israeli jails and the right of return of the refugees to their homes according to UN Resolution 194. We demand the recognition of Palestine as a full member of the UN and its respective recognition by all states. We salute the struggle of our friends from the peace-loving forces inside Israel, who face the reactionary regime and its policies while struggling side by side with the Palestinian people to end the occupation, and for social, political and people's rights in Israel.

Last but not at all least, we would like to underline the importance of one particular case of US military bases, the one on the Cuban soil at Guantánamo. It has to be said clearly that while all foreign military bases are not welcome by the peoples, the case of Guantánamo is special because in Cuba both people and government, since the triumph of the revolution on 1st January 1959, demand the closure and removal of the US base and its return to Cuba. This is even more important when we know that the USA is operating there a concentration camp for torture. We would like to highlight the important international seminar, which is the VI International Seminar for Peace and the Abolition of Foreign Military Bases, to be held in the Cuban province of Guantánamo on May 4-6, 2019, jointly organized by the Cuban Movement for Peace and the Sovereignty of the Peoples (MOVPAZ) and the WPC.

Dear Friends,

For all the above and based on our historical mandate for almost seventy years ago, we continue the history and the legacy of bravery and dedication by peace fighters and militants, who seven decades ago sought to rebuild the world with democracy, national sovereignty, social progress and peace, following the catastrophe of war and devastation and the unprecedented suffering imposed on so many peoples.

The strengthening of the struggle against imperialist wars and militarism, for peace and disarmament and for solidarity with the peoples victimized by foreign interference and aggression by imperialism, is one of the most urgent tasks of our time. It is to this struggle that the WPC remains deeply committed, with all those who defend the cause of peace and solidarity with the peoples, in a broad anti-imperialist movement.

Thank you.

Joe Lombardo
Co-Coordinator
United National Antiwar Coalition (UNAC)
USA

Historians usually point to Guantánamo as the first US foreign military base. However, technically, the historians are not correct; the US had bases outside its territory many years before that. There were bases built in the western area of US territory before it became part of the US. These were for the sole purpose of stealing land occupied by Native Americans, and eventually, these bases were used to steal as much as one-third of Mexico's territory, which today is the southwestern part of the United States.

Texas, which was called Tajas when it was part of Mexico, was also part of this land grab. There is a lot of folklore around Texas leaving Mexico and becoming part of the US. Many have learned of the "heroic" efforts of Davy Crocket and Daniel Boone at the Alamo, but the real reason that the rich landowners of Taxes wanted to leave Mexico and join the United States is because Mexico had outlawed slavery and slavery was still legal in the US.

The legacy of slavery and white supremacy has never been dealt with in the US and racism has always been used in wars to dehumanize the "enemy" to make it easier to kill them. So US soldiers learn that the "enemy" are "rag heads" or "gooks" or other racist names.

But although there were forts or bases outside of the US for many years, the real expansion of US foreign military bases did not occur until after World War II, in the period the US proclaimed the "American Century."

After WWI, the US closed its bases used to wage war and sent the soldiers home. But after WWII, they did not close the bases and did not demobilize the military. There were protests by the soldiers, who demanded to be released to go home after the war. These protests were called the "going home movement." The retention of US military bases and the refusal to demobilize the military along with the bombing of Hiroshima and Nagasaki really had little to do with WWII but were the opening salvos of the new Cold War. During the Cold War, the US and its allies tried to neutralize and destroy the Soviet Union and defeat Communism. NATO was established during this period also with that goal in mind.

However, after the fall of the Soviet Union, NATO did not dissolve but increased in size and so did the number of US foreign military bases. As the Soviet Union was collapsing, along with its allies called the Warsaw Pact countries, the US made a pledge to the Soviet leaders that it would not expand NATO into the former Soviet states or the Warsaw Pact countries but today NATO has moved into twelve of those countries and uses its bases and military in this region to surround and threaten Russia.

Today, the US has its military in about 172 countries and has about twenty times the number of foreign military bases as all of the rest of the countries of the world combined. The countries with the second and third greatest number of foreign military bases are the UK and France. These are the remnants of their own empires of the past. These two countries are also NATO allies of the US. For this reason, when we organize to close foreign military bases we must keep our focus firmly on the US and NATO bases. These are the real threats to peace in the world.

So, as we have heard at this conference, next April 4 the leaders of NATO will be coming to the US to celebrate the 70th anniversary of its founding. When they come, they will be met by the peace movement. We must mobilize to protest this NATO celebration. April 4th is also the anniversary of the killing of Dr. Martin Luther King, Jr., who was killed exactly one year after his famous speech at Riverside Church in New York where he came out against the war in Vietnam and called the US the "greatest purveyor of violence in the world."

Bringing NATO to Washington, DC on that date is an affront to everything that Martin Luther King stood for. On March 30, the Saturday before the NATO meeting, we will be holding a mass march and rally. Other activity is planned for the period between March 30 and April 4.

I hope that you will join us in Washington, DC to protest against NATO, war and racism.

Plenary 2:

Environmental and Health Impacts
of Military Bases

Chair:
Senator Grace O'Sullivan
Green Party
Ireland

Chair's Opening Remarks

Senator Grace O'Sullivan
Member of the Upper House of the Irish Parliament
Green Party, Ireland

I'm going to start the next session. I would like to begin by thanking you all for coming to Ireland, to Dublin, to participate in this conference. As you know, this is the first international conference against US and NATO military bases so it is a great opportunity to start the networking and collaboration. We have some great speakers here today, which I'll be delighted to introduce to you in a moment.

My name is Grace O'Sullivan. I am a Green Party Senator. I was a member of Greenpeace in 1985, when we scaled the US nuclear — the US military base — in a place called Kwajalein Atoll in the Marshall Islands in the Pacific Ocean, so I have a long history in the peace and justice movement. I think more than ever, today we have to consolidate, we have to have solidarity to do our utmost to oppose nuclear and military bases.

This morning's session is on the environmental and health impacts of military bases and our first speaker is Dr. Zuhal Okuyan. Dr Okuyan is the Chairwoman of the Peace Committee of Turkey, which was formerly known as the Peace Association. Dr. Zuhal is a medical doctor and a public health specialist, so I can think of no one better to talk about the environmental and health impacts of military bases. Dr. Zuhal will speak for about fifteen minutes. Then I will introduce our next speaker and then the third speaker.

Because we are assembled here today and because many of you have travelled from really far away, I think we should have a question and answer session at the end to give people the opportunity to make a very short statement and to raise questions. We will start with Dr. Zuhal.

Thank you very much.

Dr. Zuhal Okuyan
President, Peace Committee of Turkey

Friends and Comrades,

I am very glad to be here in Ireland, which has a long tradition of historical struggles.

I am the spokeswoman of the Turkish Peace Committee, which was previously known as the Peace Association of Turkey but unfortunately it was banned two years ago.

I will talk about the environmental and health-related issues arising out of the existence of NATO bases. I am a public health specialist and a medical school teacher.

Military bases harm the ecosystem, biodiversity and the health of humans and animals. First of all we must define 'health'. According to the World Health Organisation's definition: Health is a state of complete physical, mental and social well-being and not merely the absence of disease or infirmity. But is this definition enough? We should also talk about the health of the planet, protecting the biodiversity and sustainability of life. But only fighting for the environment is not enough, we must combine the environmental fight with the anti-imperialist and anti-capitalist struggle as all of these concepts are related to each other. We must not forget that our struggle is not just for enough food or for clean air. Another big mistake is to claim that only individuals are responsible for the environment. That is true up to a certain point, but I'm not responsible for global warming; you are not either. What about aircraft, for example, including military aircraft, which use special jet engine fuel? We must not forget the corporate and governmental side of the story. They want us to forget that part of the problem. They tell us that we must not eat this and must not do that to make the problem appear a matter of individual behaviour. However, the definition of health and wellbeing goes beyond that.

Military forces destroy the environment not only during war time, but their activities in so-called peace time also threaten the ecosystem seriously. This fact is known and discussed by the authorities and many armies, especially the US army, which is now trying to be 'greener' than before due to the visible pollution around military bases and to the reaction of the locals and settlers living within the bases. Over the last ten years, a new field has emerged, called "Warfare Ecology," which has already taken its place in the academic world.

The powers that pollute the military bases, especially the US, have large military bases all over the world. Most scientific research about military bases, however, has been done on US bases! We have learned many things about how chemical compounds used in military bases pollute the water and the soil.

It is not only in wartime that military activities affect the environment and health. Military activities in so-called peacetime also result in damage, including to the ecosystem everywhere. How do they do this? By polluting the water, the soil, the flora and fauna, because the installation of military bases causes harm. People are moved from their homes and forced to migrate. Trees are cut down. The environment is totally changed. Bases use a great deal of energy, including fossil fuels. So we, the people, are not responsible for global warming, but they are.

Bases need infrastructure for their employees, including barracks for soldiers. They use local resources. I'm not talking about the social problems that are caused by military bases, including crimes such as rape. I am only referring to the environmental consequences arising out of the use of chemical compounds and other hazardous substances.

How and when do the military bases cause environmental harm?

1. During the establishment: Cutting trees, spoiling farming areas.

2. During non-operational periods with full employment and equipment: Harm and pollution due to the settlements, barracks and the dense population of the bases. Use of local resources like water, waste formation, noise pollution, cultural conflicts and individual crimes. Air, soil and water pollution. Effects on the surrounding populations and farming. Fire training leads to the accumulation of the chemical substances.

3. During military operations: Military activities use lots of energy, mostly fossil energy sources (carbon emmisions). Heavy vehicle exercises (like tanks) have long-term effects on land, destroying fauna and flora. They make craters on the ground and cause soil erosion. Farmers are very much affected by such exercises. There are serious effects from military aviation; aircraf produce particles and gases, which contribute to global warming. Military jets also cause noise pollution. According to the World Health Organization (WHO), exposure to prolonged or excessive noise can cause a range of health problems ranging from stress, poor concentration, productivity loss in the workplace, and communication difficulties and fatigue from lack of sleep, to more serious issues such as cardiovascular disease, cognitive impairment, tinnitus and hearing loss. The world's military forces are responsible for the release of two thirds of chlorofluorocarbons (CFCs) into the Ozone Layer. Flight training by the military releases chemical substances that stay in the soil and water for decades causing cancers and birth defects. Another effect on nature is the mass destruction of birds.

4. Disasters (natural or accidents): Military bases are full of hazardous material, which can spread around during floods or earthquakes or serious accidents within bases may occur.

5. After abolition: Pollution is created due to oil and oil products and other toxic substances. Air, soil and water pollution may harm the people living in nearby settlements and effect farming for a long time. The biodiversity of the region may effected.

The Pentagon is responsible for releasing five times more toxins into the environment than the five US companies most responsible for polluting the world with chemicals. One may ask about international written documents and sanctions. It should be noted that military activities have been excluded from the famous Kyoto Protocol, which is very interesting.

There are two principles in the Declaration of the UN Conference on Environment and Development (UNCED) in Rio de Janeiro, which was held in 1992 ("Earth Summit"), which can be related to our subject:

Principle 24: Warfare is inherently destructive of sustainable development. Nations shall respect international laws protecting the environment in times of armed conflict, and shall cooperate in their further establishment.

Principle 25: Peace, development and environmental protection are interdependent and indivisible.

But who will protect these principles? International documents have no role of sanction in today's world of a crazy armament race.

Some examples of military bases and their environmental impacts

Camp Century in Greenland: Climate change is turning a Cold War project into an environmental hazard in Greenland as the ice melts. Camp Century was constructed in 1959, under the cover of a scientific research project of the USA, powered by a nuclear reactor, situated under the ice cover. It was in fact a military base and the planners thought that the thick ice layer would protect and hide the base. But after the first tunnels were built, it was discovered that the ice layer was not so strong and that the tunnels were not safe. After some years Camp Century was abandoned. In 2016 researchers found that there was a large amount of chemical waste there from diesel fuel and other chemical compounds like polychlorinated byphenyls (PCBs). If the melting of the ice continues, the waste will disrupt the ecosystem around the base. And Camp Century is not unique, there are many other abandoned bases all over the world.

Okinawa example: Both the Kadena and Futenma airfields in Okinawa are near crowded residential areas. Locals complain of the noise of aircraft landing and taking off. Continous noise can cause hearing loss, psychological effects and sleep disturbance.

US nuclear vessels making port calls at the White Beach installation (Katsuren Peninsula), and the firing of depleted uranium shells at Torishima Bombing Range, have given rise to concerns about the effects of radiation on the surrounding environment.

Hazardous materials like PCB's were found in the soil of US military properties returned to local owners. It was discovered that soil and groundwater were contaminated. There were also oil spills, leaks that spoil the water.

Pollution on some US bases: It was scientifically proven that many bases and surrounding areas were polluted by chemicals, including Camp Lejeune in North Carolina, Naval Air Station Fallon in Nevada, and Marine Corps Air Station El Toro in California. During the early 1980s, high concentrations of hazardous chemicals were discovered in groundwater and drinking water serving some areas at Camp Lejeune. Groundwater was contaminated with some very dangerous chemicals like TriCloroEthylene (TCE), PerCloroEthylene (PCE), benzene, toluene, ethylbenzene, and xylene. Many people were affected. Chemical compounds cause cancers and birth defects. Apart from the petroleum products, the chemical in fire-fighting foams pollutes the military base because of firefighting training Per-and polyfluoroalkyl Substances (PFAS). These can pollute the soil and water and accumulate in living organisms. These substances may lead to birth defects, effect the thyroid hormone, the immune system and may cause cancer.

We can give more examples from all over the world. I think more research should be done on this issue and we must have a network for compiling the findings.

I would like to finish by saying that as an activist and a teacher I will continue to give examples of the environmental damage caused by military bases and I will continue to talk to young people.

We must not forget who is really responsible for the environmental damage caused by military bases. We don't always see the full picture.

Thank you very much.

Milan Krajca
Chairman, Czech Peace Movement
Czech Republic

Dear Comrades and Friends,

First of all I would like to express my thanks to the organizers of this important conference — to the Irish Peace and Neutrality Alliance and to the Coalition Against U.S. Foreign Military Bases from the United States. It is a pleasure to be here on behalf of our organization, the Czech Peace Movement, from the Czech Republic. I am glad to represent here also a peace movement from Central and Eastern Europe, the region which is strongly connected with the issue of our conference.

The struggle against US foreign military bases is one of the most important issues on the agenda of the peace movement today. Foreign bases are military instruments of imperialism. They are a tool to control natural resources and trade, and are a threat of aggression and interference against peoples and nations. Seeking to assure its dominance over the world, the US maintains almost 1,000 military bases, where it stations hundreds of thousands of soldiers equipped with the most sophisticated weaponry, war planes, missiles and war ships. This represents 95% of all foreign military bases in the world, and it includes US bases in every continent and region. It is important to add that besides maintaining military bases across the world, US imperialism seeks to dominate seas and oceans through seven powerful naval fleets and to control outer and cybernetic space through an infinity of satellites, spy crafts, radar stations and communications networks.

NATO is the largest military organization in the world. It is imperialism's key military instrument. NATO is an extension of US military power and acts according to its interests. It was founded, in 1949, four years after the end of World War II and six years before the creation of the Warsaw Pact. At the beginning of the last decade of the twentieth century, the charade about its proclaimed "defensive character" became even clearer: the disappearance of the Warsaw Pact was not followed by the dissolution of NATO, but rather by its reinforcement. It is now a superstructure on a planetary scale. It is a powerful military organization, under US domain, consists of twenty-nine member states in North America and Europe and maintains diverse partnerships with dozens of countries in all continents. There is also a need to mark a deep link between NATO and the other imperialist international structure — the European Union, the European Union that declares in the Lisbon Treaty its status as the "European pillar" of NATO. From its founding days seventy years ago, NATO has been an offensive military alliance and has always been ready to intervene. NATO's expansion and provocations are directly responsible for destabilization, tensions, violence and war.

Our country, the Czech Republic, joined NATO almost twenty years ago, in 1999. It happened despite several promises made at that time, without a referendum and against the will of the majority of the Czech people. What happened after this NATO enlargement is well known. Just a few days after the Czech Republic, Poland and Hungary joined NATO, the criminal NATO bombing of Yugoslavia began. The Czech Republic, as a new NATO member state, was on the side of this barbarian aggression that we will commemorate in a few months. During the last two decades, Yugoslavia was followed by several other countries — victims of imperialist aggression supported also by our country as a NATO member state — for example, Afghanistan, Iraq, Libya, and Syria. We, the Czech Peace Movement, together with other peace, anti-war and anti-imperialist forces strongly oppose this policy of war and aggression connected to NATO and our struggle goes on.

In our struggle there was one really important victory I would like to share with you. In 2006, they published the first information about the secret negotiations between the US and Czech governments to construct a US military missile base in the Czech Republic, part of the so-called missile defence system of the USA. It refers to the system that is being developed by the United States to detect and intercept any type of missile launched from anywhere in the world and includes a network of sensors, space satellites, land and sea radars, land and sea interceptor missiles and a communications, command and control network. By being able to intercept any missile, the system ensures, in practice, a monopoly of this type of weaponry by the United States. With this system the US could launch an attack — including a nuclear one — against any country in the world, remaining safe from a possible response.

Immediately after the information about the secret negotiations between our government and the US government was published, a huge popular campaign was started against the attempt to build this so-called anti-missile base, consisting mainly of military radar. Our organization, the Czech Peace Movement, was established at that time as well as our friendly broader No to Bases initiative and several other structures. In this campaign we demanded the publication of all the documents of the secret negotiations about the plan to construct a US military base in the country, resolutely opposed this plan and asked for a referendum on this crucial issue concerning the whole country and all its inhabitants. There have been also demands to organize local referendums on the issue of the US military base in the municipalities that were potential neighbours of the base. Such a referendum was organized in some municipalities close to the area of the base where a huge majority of its inhabitants opposed the US military base plan.

We organized hundreds of public protests, demonstrations, debates with citizens and also a very successful petition under which hundreds of thousands of signatures have been gathered so far. A strong opposition mobilized public opinion in the Czech Republic where approximately 80% of the population rejected the proposal for a US military base in their country. There were hundreds of reasons for that. Among them was the possible impact of the planned military radar base on the environment and the health of citizens. For instance, a published report by leading Czech scientists suggested that the rays emitted by the radar base could pose a threat to those travelling in airplanes overhead. In this context it is important to mention that this base was planed to be built just dozens of kilometers from our capital, Prague, in Brdy forest, where nature was already significantly affected by preparatory work for the base construction.

Finally, after three years of the daily mass struggle against the installation of this US military radar base, we succeeded. In 2009, the US administration decided to cancel the plan to build a stationary radar in the Czech Republic as a part of the so-called missile defence system. One of the official reasons for the decision was the existence of a strong popular anti-base movement supported by the overwhelming majority of the population, which created significant pressure on Czech political representatives because of the demand for a referendum and to stop the building of this base. This was a really important victory for all peace-loving people in the Czech Republic, who were able to reject imperialist military plans in their country and to save the country, at least until now, from any permanent foreign military base.

This experience of our successful struggle against the attempt to install a US military base is relevant today. What we recognize now as very dangerous is a significant increase in the presence of NATO in our region, i.e., Central and Eastern Europe. There is today a debate on the construction of a huge US military base in Poland, famous Fort Trump, but there are already many US bases in our region. It is not a secret that, to increase of its permanent and semi-permanent presence in the former socialist states of Central and Eastern Europe, NATO today is also engaged in various military exercises involving tens of thousands of soldiers, which are both a military demonstration and a provocation.

For instance one of them, the military exercise Saber Strike, which takes place every year in the Baltic States, demonstrates the increase in the number of NATO soldiers participating there: in 2014, 4,700 soldiers; in 2015, 6,000 soldiers; in 2016, 10,000 soldiers; in 2017, 11,000 soldiers; and, finally, in 2018, 18,000 soldiers. And this exercise was definitely not the only one that took place in the Baltics this year. There was at the same time the Baltops exercise of the US Navy in the Baltic Sea, and the Footprint 18, an exercise of special operations forces, which brought 2,000 special operations personnel to the Baltic States officially to test a situation of hybrid war under conditions of a real armed conflict.

Speaking about numbers, the biggest exercise this year and one of the biggest in NATO history was the two-week-long Trident Juncture NATO drill in Norway with the participation of around 50,000 troops. Another significant military exercise that should be mentioned was the Anaconda exercise, which took place this year in Poland, with the participation of 31,000 soldiers, 5,000 military vehicles and more than 150 aircraft. Since 2014 and the Maidan coup in the Ukraine, NATO has reinforced its presence in that country and in the Black Sea area. There have been, for instance, military exercises Rapid Trident, Sea Breeze and Sea Shield with the participation of thousands of US/NATO soldiers.

The US say that their enlarged military presence in our region is to secure our so-called "independence, democracy, freedom," etc. But the reality is very clear: they are there to maintain mainly their dominance and to prepare for a war, a war we have to stop.

As a proud member organization of the World Peace Council, we are participating in its international campaign "YES TO PEACE! NO TO NATO!" We demand a Czech Republic without foreign military troops, an end to the participation of the Czech Army abroad in various imperialist military missions, for instance in Afghanistan or in the Baltic. We oppose the pressure of US imperialism to increase military budgets to 2% of GDP, and generally we struggle against our country's membership in NATO. Our goal is to change Czech foreign policy to be based on independence and peace.

To conclude, there are two important military tools of imperialism — the network of foreign military bases and NATO. In our region of the former socialist states of the Central and Eastern Europe, we unfortunately have experience of both of them. But on the other hand, we in the Czech Republic also have experience from our struggle against the attempt to build a US foreign military base in our country, when we were able to confront imperialist plans, and we succeeded. This experience is very important today, when we have to struggle against a further increase in the US' and NATO's military presence in our region, and I am proud to have had an opportunity to share it with you.

Thank you very much.

Pat Elder
Civilian Exposure, World BEYOND War
USA

I ran for Congress in the recent election as a Green Party candidate for an area in Maryland south of Washington DC and I received 1.3% of the vote. I ran against Steny Hoyer, who is second in line in the Democratic Party, and who received 71% of the vote. I was fortunate to raise $100 a day for six months during the campaign. My opponent raised $100,000 a day for six months. In the US, we have extremely high levels to which you can contribute to the political process. In his career, Hoyer has raised $80 million but most of the money he has received has come from chemical companies and the military companies like Lockheed Martin, for instance, or Raytheon or Northrop. So that is what we are up against but, hey, I'm going to run again.

I'm a political activist, not a scientist, but I've been researching this issue thoroughly for several years.

I'm going to pronounce the names of some chemicals. I'm a political activist, not a scientist, but I've been researching this issue thoroughly for several years. PFOA and PFAS are two of the most deadly. These compounds are no laughing matter. They're killing us.

A study was produced by the Pentagon earlier this year after tremendous pressure over years and years. They were forced to show their cards. They tested several thousand wells at US bases and most are polluted by these compounds. The DOD has identified 401 bases in the US with groundwater contaminated by PFAS, along with nine bases overseas.

Just read that please. The stuff is deadly and mostly affects women and their reproductive health all over the world.

Few connected the dots until the Pentagon Report came out and people began to publish things on Facebook such as "I had a miscarriage." There were references to 300 miscarriages on one Facebook page, all having occurred at navy bases or air force bases throughout the United States.

Kate Kelly was approached by the press after posting something on Facebook. She said "you can quote me." Women are rising up. Kate Kelly is speaking out.

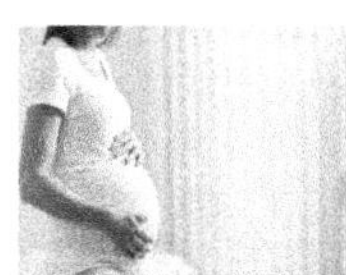

Water is still poisoned and people are still drinking the water.

Kate drank the water. And notice that last line, "When you're stateside you certainly don't expect toxic exposure."

Don't get pregnant. She did and miscarried.

[Prolonged silence]

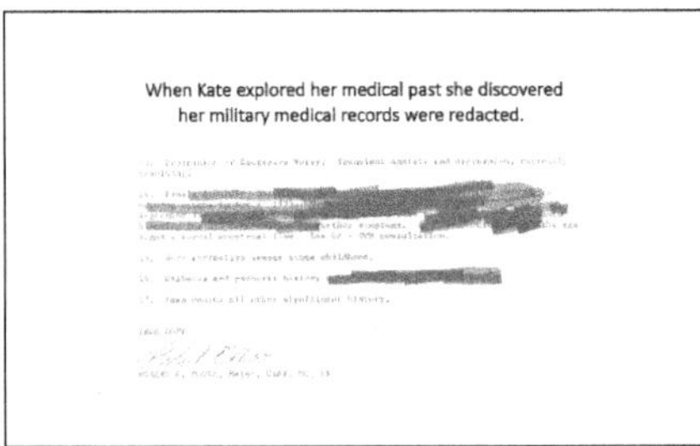

[Prolonged silence]

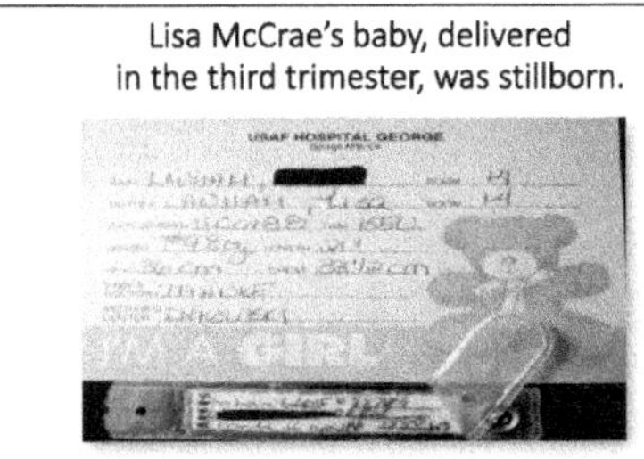

Water samples taken in 2018 showed water 5,396 parts per trillion (ppt) above the 70 ppt limit for these carcinogens.

They weren't counting on Facebook.

They purged everything.

"I keep getting the run around. It's like they aren't able to provide anything at this time."

In 2018 a well in the community close to the base tested for 3,300 ppt for PFOA. Harvard scientists say 1 ppt may be dangerous to human health. These are known as "the forever chemicals."

Beautiful — It looks like a jigsaw puzzle, but it's contaminated by Pease Air Force Base.

1,500 had their blood tested and they've all been poisoned. They're anxious about their future.

U.S. Sen. Jeanne Shaheen represents Portsmouth and she is standing up to the military on PFAS.

At Pease AF Base in Portsmouth NH, PFAS levels were found to be at 870 ppt, more than ten times the EPA limit of 70 ppt. "We have 1,500 people who have been tested with elevated levels in the Portsmouth area, who are anxious about their future and their children's future. And I know there are many people throughout the Air Force and our other military installations who share that concern," said Sen. Jeanne Shaheen, D-New Hampshire in April of 2018.

Just read it. Only 6 US Senators have had the guts to confront the military by supporting this common sense first step measure, while their constituents are being poisoned.

Just six U.S. Senators have the guts to confront the military while their constituents are being poisoned. In April, Shaheen introduced S. 2719 to direct the Secretary of Veterans Affairs to establish a registry to ensure that members of the Armed Forces who may have been exposed to PFAS and PFAO on military installations receive information regarding such exposure. It's a radical measure!

Andrew Wheeler, Scott Pruitt's replacement is no improvement. They are foxes in charge of the hen house. Since the Dublin conference, Michael Dourson has been identified as someone the DOD is interviewing to defend their ongoing practice of using PFAS in fire fighting foams.

Murderous Bastards

July 19, 2017 - Trump nominates Michael Dourson, a chemical industry insider as EPA Assistant Administrator in charge of regulating the chemical industry. Dourson advocates for radically relaxed EPA standards concerning PFAS.

October 18, 2017 – EPA chief Pruitt installs Dourson, defying the Senate's constitutional authority

Dec. 13, 2017 – Senate rejects Dourson nomination, citing his record as a chemical industry insider attempting to lessen regulations on PFAS.

Jan. 25, 2018 – Dourson leaves his job at the EPA.

Belgium. There's a lot of work to be done protecting these innocent people while filling them with a sense of righteous indignation against the perpetrators of this criminal activity.

DOD's Contaminated Water Database (March, 2018) lists 401 bases with PFAS and PFAO poisoned water. Nine foreign bases are on the list which shows concentrations of the contaminants in part per trillion. Over 70 ppt is unsafe.

- Army Soto Cano AB, HN Honduras 72.5- 82.9
- Army USAG Daegu, KR Camp Carroll Korea 76- 1,066
- Army USAG Daegu, KR Camp Walker Korea 91- 789
- Army USAG Red Cloud, KR: Camp Red Cloud Korea 171- 466
- Army USAG Red Cloud, KR: Camp Stanley Korea 80- 1,061
- **Army USAG Benelux - Caserne Daumerie, BE Belgium 84-94**
- Navy NSF Diego Garcia Diego Garcia 77-5,849
- Navy - BRAC Agana Guam PFOA + PFOS combined = 88 - 410
- Air Force - Kunsan AB South Korea 1 1 55-85 ppt

The water is unsafe to drink in Belgium.

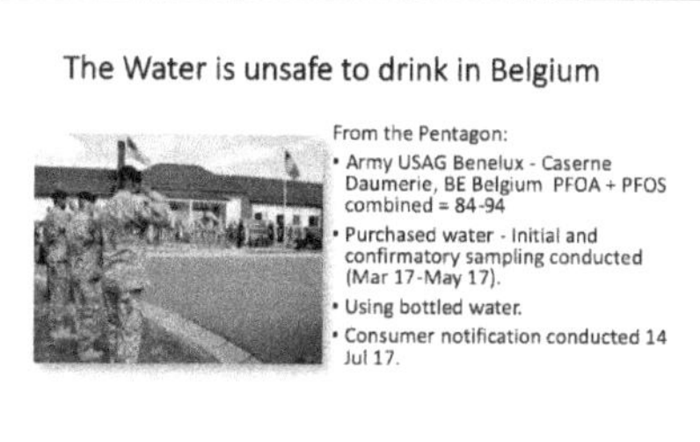

"Unfortunately, the Air Force hasn't acted and that's why I'm writing."

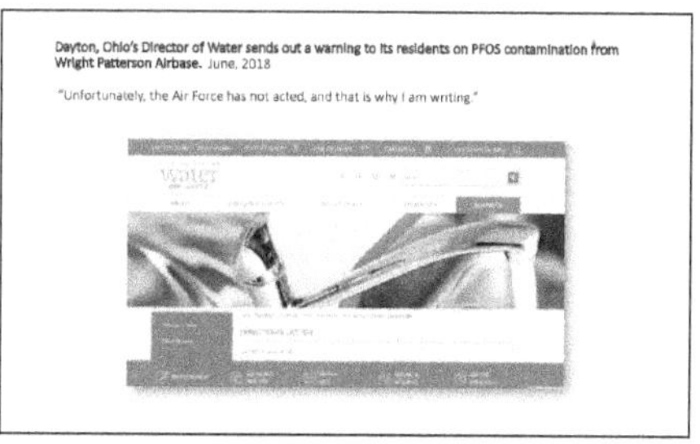

Wurtsmith Air Force Base in Michigan was closed 25 years ago and the water in the surrounding communities is still poisoned. PFOS and PFOA are known as the forever chemicals.

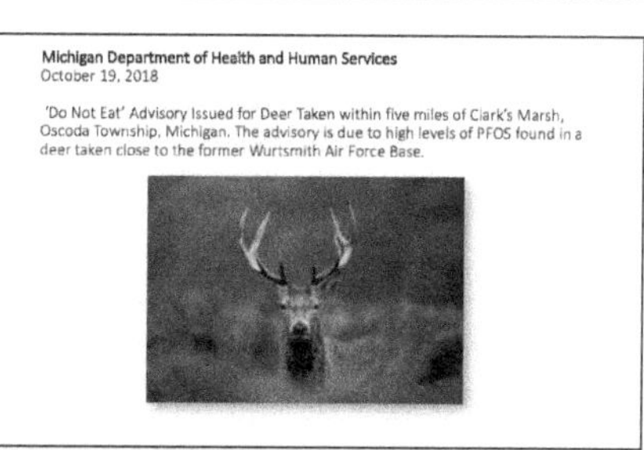

Just read it. The Envionmental Protection Agency still does not regulate these chemicals.

The lying bastards claimed "other sources likely contaminated the water."

The Air Force refuses to reimburse three Colorado communities for the money spent responding to water poisoned by PFAS and PFAO used in firefighting foam at Peterson Air Force Base. The poor towns have an $11 million tab. The water in El Paso County, Texas is unsafe to drink.

The Air Force claimed other sources likely contributed to the aquifer's contamination, though none has been identified. The sons of bitches.

Plenary 3:

Central and South America / Guantánamo

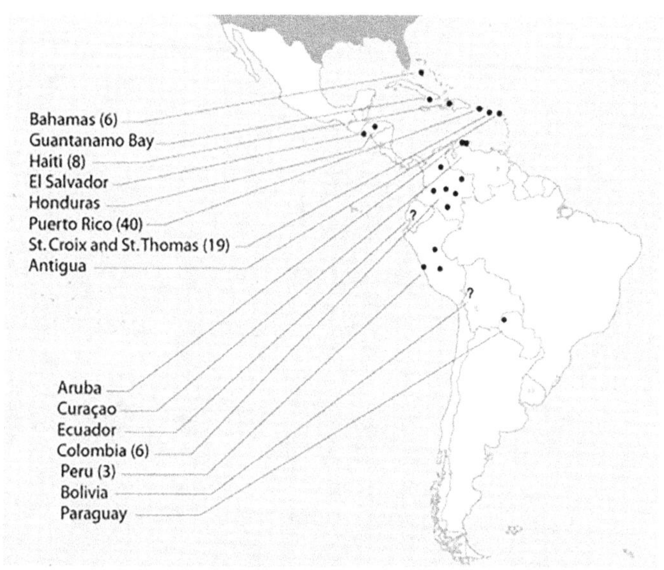

Chair:
James Patrick Jordan
Alliance for Global Justice
USA

Chair's Opening Remarks

James Patrick Jordan
Co-Coordinator, Alliance for Global Justice
USA

Dia daoibh agus fáilte! Hello, and welcome!

It is appropriate that we convene this panel in Ireland, given its long history of solidarity with Latin America in its struggle against Empire. William Lampart of Wexford was executed in 1659 because he fought for the abolition of slavery and the freedom of Mexico. The Chilean independence leader, Bernardo O'Higgins, was a man of Irish extraction. Here's to Saint Patrick's Battalion, Irish soldiers in the US army who joined their Mexican comrades in the resistance to foreign invasion by the United States during the US-Mexico War. And I would be remiss not to mention Ireland's Colombia Three, who were jailed in Bogotá in the US-funded La Modelo Prison for the crime of studying Colombia's struggle for peace and liberation.

There was a time in Latin America when the movement against foreign US military bases was in the ascendancy. But today what we see are setbacks. The governments in Brazil, Argentina, Peru, and Honduras have all turned over territory for new US bases. Colombia, with seven such bases, has officially become the very face of NATO in Latin America, and has even sent troops to Yemen, Afghanistan, and Western Africa.

Permanent US bases are only one component of the Empire's foreign military infrastructure. Large exercises to deploy temporary, mobile bases are justified as preparations for humanitarian and disaster interventions. What they really are, are rehearsals for regime change aimed at Venezuela, Cuba, Nicaragua, and Bolivia.

The reactivation of the Fourth Naval Fleet in the Caribbean is yet another component.

The militarized border is a new kind of base, imposing martial law and domestic occupation in the US, clearly directed at our southern neighbors as well as inwardly. As we speak, over 5,000 US troops have been sent to allegedly defend against a caravan of desperate refugees displaced by US neoliberal policies.

But let me proclaim clearly: Empire, your days are numbered.

Tiochfaidh ar lá! ¡Nuestro día vendrá! Our day will come!

Silvio Platero
President
Cuban Movement for Peace and Sovereignty
of the Peoples (MOVPAZ)
Cuba

The Armed Forces of the United States today have the largest number of personnel and military installations outside their borders. Data updated in February of this year, 2018, indicate that US personnel in active military service amount to more than 1.4 million men and women, of whom about 350,000 are deployed abroad in more than 150 countries, including the diplomatic military personnel and personnel for the protection of embassies. The main combat forces, however, are stationed in more than 800 military installations located in forty-two countries, of which 181 are in Germany, 122 in Japan, about 100 in Italy and eighty-three in South Korea.

It is necessary to specify that in the political-military circles of the United States, for several years they have been changing the language to denominate the military bases that they have abroad, with the objective of diminishing the denunciations of the social and pacifist movements in the struggle against the bases and military installations.

In this way, US politicians and the military usually say that in Latin America and the Caribbean, for example, they have a single military base in Guantánamo Bay, and the rest are simply medium and small facilities. This claim must be rejected strongly in our struggle against foreign military presence. At present, it is known that in the Caribbean region there are seventy-six US bases and military installations. Some specialists on the subject suggest that there could be 100.

Next, we highlight the military presence in the region — Latin America and the Caribbean. From the point of view of the military-political doctrine, the general guidelines are clearly reflected in a recent document of the US Southern Command entitled "Strategy of Military Operations Theater 2017–2021" where it is proposed that:

"The United States and the region share a wide range of interests. In 2016, US trade with Central and South America exceeded 200 million dollars. Today, more than 18 percent of our citizens have Hispanic roots, of whom 27.3 million are eligible to vote in 2016.

"These demographics are shaping the future of the United States, these factors — strategic, economic and cultural — reinforce the deep ties of the United States with the region."

Likewise, it points out the following as the main challenges facing our region:

— Transregional and transnational illicit networks.
— Natural disasters and the outbreak of infectious diseases, which are aggravated by poverty and ungovernability (generate instability, migration, etc.).
— The greater presence of China, Russia and Iran in the region.

"These challenges will be addressed through a Network of Networks," operated by the Southern Command in conjunction with the US agencies and the allies and partner nations, through a combination of diplomacy, development and defense. This network includes agencies and networks of the US government; the networks of allied and coparticipating nations; networks of civil society, the academic sector, the private sector and populations that extend governance."

The effort of the Theater Campaign Plan will focus among other issues on developing a greater capacity to face contingencies: "Manage the first seventy-two hours of chaos in any circumstance.... If necessary we must be prepared to run it alone, until additional help arrives."

The response in cases of contingencies includes:

— Defense of the Panama Canal and the Panama Canal Area.
— Migration Control Operations.
— Humanitarian Assistance and Disaster Response (including response to epidemics).
— Unilateral, Bilateral or Multilateral Military Operations carried out by the forces in response to any crisis.

The Southern Command of the United States, whose area of responsibility covers our entire region, is composed of:

— The Southern Army located at Fort Sam, Houston, Texas.
— The Southern Air Force, located at the Davis Air Force Base in Monthan, Arizona.
— The South Naval Forces Command located at the Naval Base of Mayport, Florida, headquarters of the US Fourth Fleet.
— The South Marine Corps Forces established in Miami, Florida.
— The Southern Special Operations Command that serves the Homestead Air Reserve Base, near Miami, Florida.

The main military installations are:

Main Operational Base (MOB):

— Guantánamo Naval Base, Cuba, where the Joint Task Force Guantánamo and the Detention Fields of the Base are located, with 807 men.

Forward Operational Site (FOS):

— Enrique Soto Cano Airport in Palmerola, Honduras, where 384 hombres are stationed.

Emplacement of Cooperative Security (CSL):

— International Airport Reina Beatrix, Aruba, Netherlands jusrisdiction (20 men).
— International Airport Hato, Curaçao, Dutch Antiles, the Netherlands, (23 effectives).

— International Airport Comalapa, El Salvador (43 hombres).

Emplacements of Cooperative Security in Colombia (with more than 600 military men)

— Air Base Palanquero, Cundinamarca Departament, Colombia (the United States invested \$42 million for the improvement of the runway and the facilities).
— Air Base Apiay, Meta Departament, Colombia.
— Air Base Malambo, Atlántico Departament, Colombia.
— Military Base Larandia, Caquetá Departament, Colombia.
— Military Base Tolemaida, Tolima Departament, Colombia.
— Naval Base Bolívar, Cartagena de Indias, Bolívar Departament, Colombia (Caribbean Sea).
— Naval Base Mágala, Málaga Bay, Valle del Cauca Departament, Colombia (Pacific Ocean).

At the end of 2017, total active US military personnel in countries that are independent from the United States (not including Canada) — including military diplomatic personnel — was 1,800 men.

French Military Presence in Latin America, the Caribbean Sea and French Guyana

— Third Foreign Regiments of Infantry in Korou, French Guyana
— Ninth Regiment of Infantry of Marina in Cayenne, French Guyana
— Gendarmerie, French Guyana
— Adapted Overseas Military Service

Caribbean Sea

— 41st Infantry Batallion of Marina in Guadalupe
— 33rd Infantry Regiment of Marina in Martinique

British Military Presence in Latin America

— Malvinas Islands (Argentina): 1,010 active personnel.

Gunantánamo Naval Base in Our History

This base has a record that is hard to beat. It is the oldest military enclave in the United States outside its borders and the only one that exists against the will of the government where it is located.

One hundred and twelve years of illegal occupation, provocations, aggression and the deaths of valuable Cuban soldiers guarding its borders and acting as a jumping off point for invasions of other countries make up its embarrassing record. The record also includes the humiliation of native workers who work in the enclave, corruption and prostitution to satisfy the US Marines.

It also has a history of serious ecological dysfunction caused to an extraordinary bay of deep water: economic effects on the zone and enormous psychological damage to its inhabitants by the maneuvers in the base, the noise of its airplanes and the limitations on the movement and security imposed by proximity to an enemy military base.

Cuba demands the return of the national territory illegally occupied by the Guantánamo Naval Base as one of the essential principles that mark the normalization process of its relations with the United States.

It is impossible to establish a new relationship between Cuba and the US, based on the recognition of its deep divergences, as long as the Guantánamo Naval Base, the blockade and the subversion against Cuba subsist.

The illegal usurpation of part of Cuban territory is an unfriendly act that contradicts the current public discourse of the US government as of December 17. It does not correspond to the aspiration of good neighbors to overcome the old adversarial relations of the past many years, as the US Secretary of State, John Kerry, said at the reopening of the US Embassy in Havana. Hours later at a press conference, Kerry himself clarified the position of his government: Guantánamo is not at the negotiating table.

It also ignores the firm position of the Community of Latin American and Caribbean States (CELAC), as set out in the Proclamation of Latin America and the Caribbean as a Zone of Peace approved at the Second Summit of Havana in January 2014 and in the Communiqué of the XIII Meeting of National Coordinators of said regional integration mechanism held in Quito, Ecuador, from August 26 to 28, 2015.

The closure of Guantánamo and the return of the usurped territory is in the interest of the peoples of the United States and Cuba. The pettiness of the nationalism of US imperialism must give way to justice, respect for human rights, international law and the just sovereign claim of the island.

The pressure exerted by the best US children with the movement of solidarity with Cuba in other parts of the world will clear the way and tip the balance of history to make Guantánamo a territory free of foreign military and the expression of the total recovery of Cuban national sovereignty.

Paola Renata Gallo Peláez
President, The Movement for Peace, Sovereignty and Solidarity
among the Peoples of Argentina (MEPASSOL)
Argentina

Dear Brothers and Sisters,
Fighters for Peace in the World,

Thank you for inviting the Movement for Peace, Sovereignty and Solidarity among Peoples (MOPASSOL) to represent the southern corner of South America in this first conference against US/NATO military bases.

To start with, we would like to thank the Irish people for their solidarity towards our peoples, who are striving to achieve freedom, serenity, decolonisation and peace.

I want to remember today those Irishmen and women, who took part in the independence process in our America together with Simon Bolívar and José San Martín. I would like to remember today Sean O'Ryan, who was the Dean of San Martin and who helped liberate Chile and Peru. Francis Burdett O'Connor was a senior officer in Bolívar's campaigns in Peru and Bolivia. I would like to remember them, the well known, and the thousands of invisible but essential Irishmen and women. As the Cuban poet says: "That embraced our cause, our revolutionary cause." Thank you. Our eternal thanks to all of them.

These histories of solidarity are witness to the deep ties between our peoples in order to achieve a better world. A world without colonialism, that we are still trying to achieve. Thank you, and stand with us.

We are living in interesting times and in difficult times. There is no world order now. The world is being transformed, rapidly, and is becoming a place we do not know. It is a world in which the water is going to be depleted and non-renewable natural resources also, a world which is in conflict as we witness the trade war that the United States is waging with China. And facing this conflict, the United States has proclaimed its moral doctrine towards Latin America in the official declarations of the current US Secretary of State, Mike Pompeo, and his immediate predecessor, Rex Tillerson. Pompeo is a former Director of the CIA and Tillerson was Chief Executive Officer of Exxon Mobil from 2006 to 2016.

According to data from the World Bank in 2013, in the first decade of the 21st century, the so-called populist governments in South America moved one hundred million people out of poverty. They tried to do more. They created space for Latin American unity in which serenity and peace would be the goals.

After the heroic scream of "no" to the Free Trade Agreement, the alliance for free trade in the Americas, in the Fourth Summit in Mar del Plata, Argentina, in 2005, the impire deployed all the counteroffensive and launched psychological warfare, media warfare, judicial warfare, trying to delegitimize the men and women that were leaders in Latin American — a *coup d'état*, a new type of *coup d'état*, to put an end to the experiences of this popular government for good.

Coup d'état in Hondoras, in Paraguay, in Brazil, at the same time there has been a deployment of military bases from United States throughout the continent using "humanitarian" assistance and support for initiatives to tackle drug trafficking as an excuse for setting up these bases.

The forces of NATO, with the United States leading them, have deployed a terror force never seen before in the history of humankind, in order to guarantee the supremacy that is required for the security of the United States and its allies. Their influence is not only military. They are aiming to achieve global domination; not only in our territory, but also in our minds, in our hearts, in our bodies. They are trying to empower the most lethal weapon known to mankind, the atomic bomb, in human minds, through neo colonialism.

And this is making our peoples vote against their own interests when they elect right wing fascist governments and give legitimacy to the occupation by NATO forces, and the occupation by the United States, of our countries. There is a war that is being fought in our minds and for control over us by the American military.

Admiral Kurt Tidd is the current commander of the US Southern Command. In February of this year, he outlined to the United States Congress the scenarios planned for the continent, the goals and the strategies, and he said, "in terms of geographic proximity, trade, migration and culture," there is no power in the world that has a higher impact on the life of United States than Central America, South America, and the Caribbean." This is a declaration of war.

An army officer and analyst, from the United States, said recently when he was explaining the strategy of the moral coup that the imperial wants to give to the popular processes in Latin America: "in order to achieve a mobilisation from the population in trying to achieve the goals that we want, we have to be able to communicate successively what is right and what is wrong. We have to be able to generate imbalance, individual imbalance and social imbalance."

He continued: "We need to try to bias the minds of the adversity through the spreading ambiguity to attack and to mislead people which will create a massive dissection and this dissection will be physical and non physical. The goal of virtual war is about nothing short of social control. We have to conquer the enemy without having to wage a war. General Charles Wald, North American General, Pentagon Advisor, the concept of love affair; which is a tactic to use law, to use the law, as a means to achieve a military goal. It means transforming legal codes, turning them into bullets. The love affair is less lethal. It is more economical. But very often in many instances it is more efficient than just planned military actions. The principles come from trying to give legality to what is exceptional, to what is harassment and prosecution."

"It is alien to the democratic system because it is used as a substitute of the democratic system. This system chooses who is going to take part in the system and who is not, who is going to be excluded and who is going to be inside. It is promoting media assassination through legal means. A legal sentence is not important. What does matter is the path that has been taken. It may seem innocent, maybe that person is going to be innocent, but the investigation, the pressing charges, have to be on the media, has to be the highlight of all the mass media in order to (inaudible) someone and link of the leader with the more disadvantaged social moments. This is where we have to invest the most, invest, this is where we have to invest the most. We have to communicate more and we have to invest in communications and in social media."

I would like to highlight something about what MOPASSOL is trying to achieve in the field of communications and social media.

Since Mauricio Macri's government came to power, Argentina has signed military agreements with the United States, the United Kingdom and Israel. These three agreements are very important. But no doubt the one that they are most ashamed of is the one signed with the United Kingdom. It cannot even be acknowledged because it is an agreement that co ordinates military activity with the occupying force in the Falklands Islands (Islas Malvinas) and the South Sandwich and Georgia Islands.

If you want to know the terms of the agreements with the United States and Israel and the terms of the detailed agreement with the United Kingdom, I can leave them here. MOPASSOL wrote a report on them so I can move on to other subjects. Before Mauricio Macri's ascent to power, Argentina only had a NATO military base in the Falkland Islands but now we have two more bases, which have been acknowledged by the Government.

So we are talking about seventy-six major bases which our colleague and comrade, Lusani from MOPASSOL, has mentioned in a book called *Territories under Surveillance* and you can find it in an e-book. So there are now two more bases that can be added to that long list. The first base is in the province of Misiones, which has a water supply. It is one of the most important water reservoirs in the world, thanks to its ability to recharge. There is a plan to tackle drug trafficking, but we know very well that when someone says there is a plan to tackle drug trafficking it leads to is violence, killings and massive violations of human rights, which have now brought thousands of people to the border of the US, who are trying to find a better place they can call home.

The other base is in the Province of Neuquén. Oil and gas were recently discovered there, at Vaca Muerta, which has made Argentina important geopolitically. And it is not by chance that, at the same time as the base was established, the Provincial Government in Neuquén was promoting, on social media, the offices of the Southern Commander talking about their great investment in the province. This base is very close to Vaca Muerta and, as well, is very close to the airport. It has no landing strip but they don't need a landing strip anymore because they now have governments that are supporting them.

There is more food and energy in the South Atlantic. The other oceans have already been depleted, which means the South Atlantic is highly important for humankind. Indeed it is essential. The occupiers of our islands in the South Atlantic are selling licences to pirate ships that will rob our resources. We have to protect humankind. This is a reservoir of food and energy and it has to be maintained properly. We have to concern ourselves in a proper way because the future, the food supply is in the South Atlantic.

The future of Antarctica is also important. We could spend days talking about it. It is the Pandora's Box of the future of humankind.

I would like to finish with some thoughts about our big concern as activists who are trying to achieve peace. What we are trying to do is defend the world that we are going to leave to our children but most of the time our children are on the Internet! The Internet is changing how our minds work. We don't know to what extent the debates about trying to achieve a better world should be on the Internet but we need to be there too. We need to be on social media and we need to debate there. We need to fight our cultural battles on the Internet, on the world-wide-web.

The people of the world wake up every day fighting for a better world. To make this possible we have to enter the world of the Internet. We should be in the web world. So I want to ask you to help us with two incentives: First to create a school for peace. We need to train the trainers, the teachers, because they are going to train the minds of the people. The teachers want to talk about peace but they don't know how. They need tools. This is a very important concept but it is not very clear. Our civilisation has never spoken about peace. We need to teach our teachers. We need to teach them how to talk about peace.

Secondly, we need to setup a communications network. That is urgent. It is a very pressing need. We dream of a peaceful world and we are the ones that have to get working with our hands, our minds and our hearts.

A final point. MOPASSOL is campaigning to make the 9th of August the International Day of Crimes against Humankind. We have chosen that date to remember the terrible day the atomic bomb was first dropped on Japan. We want you to take part in the campaign. The campaign's tea shirt is the same colour as the tea shirt worn by the inmates of Guantánamo. So please join us in our campaign. Help us to establish that day as a day for the fighters for peace.

Thank you very much.

Myriam Parada Avila
Executive Director, School of Peace Foundation
Colombia

Good afternoon. I want to begin by saying that it is an honour to be here. It is a learning experience. As Silvio and other colleagues said, there are things we still don't know the scope of. We don't know how many military bases are there in the world, for example.

I will start with talking about the peace in Columbia.

During 2006, after a great four year-long effort and dialogue between The Revolutionary Armed Forces of Colombia — People's Army (FARC) and the Columbian Government, the Peace Agreement was signed. The Columbian people were full of hope. We were really happy with this achievement in spite of all of the difficulties, in spite of all of the sabotage, but we were really surprised when the year after President Santos put the Agreement to the people of Columbia for approval it was rejected. Here we have to talk about the role of the media. They satanized and vilified the Agreement. I might also mention the role of the Christian churches, which vilified the Agreement. They made the people feel shameful, embarrassed and angry towards the agreement. They managed to get those who were not at the centre of the war to vote against the Agreement. Those who were in the middle of the war did want the Agreement.

It is a paradox, but our country continues building peace. We take all the opportunities we can. We scream no more war and yes to life. We do not want more selective murders. We do not want the murders that have happened — 365 of them after the peace agreement. But I know, we know, there have been many more but the media will not talk about them. We demand the right to life and respect for human rights.

The Columbian people continue to be mobilised for their right to education and health. They want solutions to their problems that we have in the country. The Government has not been listening to us. They have not been providing the services. They have not been paying attention to their obligations, to their duties. The Columbian Government does not want to accept that there are paramilitary people in our country. There are paramilitaries but they will not admit it, they will not acknowledge it. We do not understand how we can sign a peace agreement while at the same time they are trying to negotiate with NATO behind everyone's backs?

The road ahead looks very uncertain but maybe not as uncertain because in the middle of all of this difficult situation the Columbian people are mobilising; students, trade unionists, embers of social organisations, even other leaders who continue to fight for peace are persecuted and murdered. We denounce the systematic murder of social leaders. I want all the peace organisations to pronounce themselves against it, so that we can build true peace with social justice and equality in our country.

I will now try to contextualise and give the background to the "seven," — as our colleague said "they're nine" — military bases in our country. It all started with Plan Columbia in 2009. It is supposed to be humanitarian aid for the country to eradicate drugs. It was signed by Álvaro Uribe's Government with President Barack Obama in 2009. They established seven military bases as a result in our land, in our country. We had a PowerPoint presentation but we'll leave it with the organisers.

I am going to talk about each one of those bases. Palanquero, for example, is an air base. It has a landing strip of 3,500m and it is the biggest US military stronghold in Latin America. It is important because it has a rapid deployment approach. Apiay, in the Departamento of Meta, is another one. It has ramps, landing strips, similar to those of Palanquero, and has great strategic value. It is there for controlling the area of the Amazon and the Orinoco basins. Barranquilla in the Departamento of the Atlántic was established to protect combat planes. Bahía Malaga in the Pacific coast. Cartagena, a naval base in the Caribbean Coast. Third parties and intelligence agents from Israel are based there, for example. Along with Palanquero and Apiay they have a protective circle around Bogotá, the capital of the country. In the Amazon region they have avant-garde technology for collecting intelligence with satellites — C-27 Orion P-3 are some of the latest generation planes.

There is a school for special rural forces, where command groups of special forces of the Yankees elite operate. They are connected to Fort Benning, Georgia, where the School of the Americas is based. Long-distance patrols are also based there, and they work with British and Israeli forces.

A professor from the University of Bogotá, who is part of the historical mission for victims of the conflict, describes Columbia as a "protector of the United States, as a servant of the United States."

In 2009, it was announced that the United States would establish seven bases, through an agreement, on the territory of Columbia. In a newspaper I read the headline "Military bases in Columbia point towards Venezuela" and that is the strategy, to corral the progressive governments that are in the way of the Empire. They are all military bases of the United States in Columbia and they are creating a strategic arc in case of a possible intervention against the Venezuelan State or Venezuelan territory. The objective is to stage a military intervention in Venezuela, overthrow Nicolás Maduro and frustrate the Bolivarian Revolution with the social changes that come with it. They will have assault troops from North American bases and the operation centre will be the biggest foreign facility in Honduras. The intervention plan against Venezuela is contained in a long document of the Southern Command of the United States, which is called "Operation Venezuela Freedom Two."

Speaking about NATO we must remember that, in 2013, former President Santos initiated the dialogue to become a member of NATO. It is said that it is only to exchange information but it is not specified what type of information. The Congress of the Republic supported that in 2014 but the Prosecutor General asked for the General Court to clarify what kind of information is going to be exchanged. In 2015 the Constitutional Court stopped it.

Despite that, an agreement that makes Columbia a global member of NATO was signed in Brussels on May 31st of this year. So, a very well designed plan was very cleverly executed behind the back of the people of Columbia.

I have to point out the importance of the role of the media. None of these issues are discussed by the media. In trade unions and social organisations we do talk about it. They are the people who try to follow what is happening in the country, to monitor it. We live in a country that is invaded. It is under invasion, a country full of military bases. It was on these bases with a high number of North American military and civil personnel that Plan Columbia was developed, which has led to our people, our women, our children becoming victims of the most abhorrent rapes, attacks, and child prostitution.

What is going to happen to our country, which is now considered the Israel of South America? It is embarrassing and shameful. But I love my country because I know there are brave people in it, because I know there are people who are thinking of building peace not only for us as a country but for the whole world.

Thank you very much.

Plenary 4:

Asia Pacific / Pivot to Asia / Okinawa

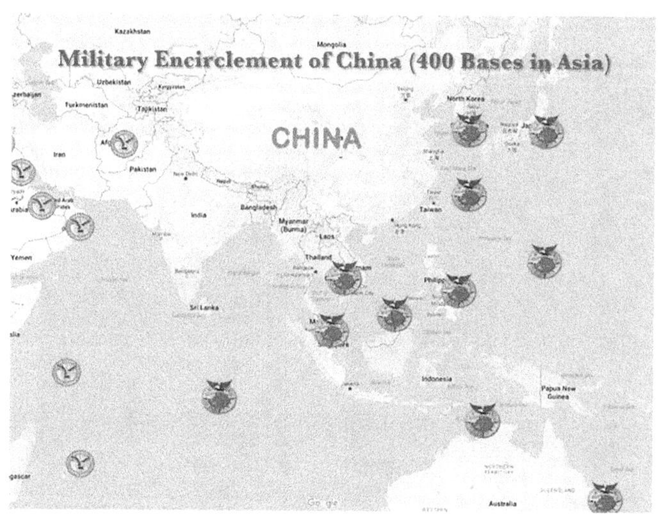

Chair:
Annette Brownlie
Independent and Peaceful Australia
Network (IPAN)
Australia

Chair's Opening Remarks

Annette Brownlie
Chairperson, Independent and Peaceful Australia
Network (IPAN)
Australia

Thank you for inviting me to this important international conference to provide an Australian peace movement perspective on the US military presence and influence in the Australian South East Asian and Pacific region of the world.

The national peace network I represent, Independent and Peaceful Australia Network or IPAN, was formed following the announcement that Australia had signed a force posture agreement with the US to host Marines on a rotational basis in Darwin at the very north of Australia.

In 2011 the Labor government agreed to the "permanent rotation of US marines and US air force aircraft", meaning we have a constant flow of US soldiers on the ground in Australia. There are currently 1,500, but this will rise to 2,500 in the near future.

It was this development that triggered the establishment of the Independent and Peaceful Australia Network (IPAN) in 2012.

Some of the world's best fighters and bombers, and Osprey hybrid aircraft, now regularly fly into Darwin and nearby Shoal Bay Receiving Station and RAAF Tindal in Katherine, with huge ships coming down from a US base in Okinawa, Japan.

The purpose is officially for training, but it is clear a much greater US military presence has been established with the navy, air-force and ground forces active throughout the year with the capability for operational action in the region.

Darwin as you can see from the map, is geographically part of the tropical South East Asian (SEA) region. Darwin has a very unique population mix with its proximity to South East Asia resulting in various ethnic communities established from countries such as Indonesia, East Timor, the Philippines and China. Darwin also has the highest percent of indigenous people in Australia at 10%. As a recent visit to Darwin showed, the appalling poverty amongst our first people is all too obvious.

Since 2011, IPAN has developed into a national network of over fifty organisations and a rising number of individual members. We have held four national conferences and are planning the 2019 conference to be held in Darwin.

The Australian American Alliance (AAA) is a more accurate description of the military and political relationship with the US, instead of the original military alliance known as ANZUS as New Zealand (NZ) withdrew from the Alliance after prohibiting any vessels holding nuclear weapons.

In my opinion, New Zealanders carry a national confidence lacking in Australia as a result of this independent David and Goliath stance in the 1980s when NZ's policy of no nuclear armed or powered ships came into force.

This map shows the extent of the US military presence in Australia. Most well known of course is Pine Gap, which I am sure most of you are aware of.

As to the political climate in Australia regarding war/militarisation and independence, the Australian Labor Party and the Conservative Coalition share most of the votes at election time; however there is a predicted change of government in 2019 to the Labor party. The Australian Greens represent around 12% of the votes.

Whilst both major political parties are 'joined at the hip' on foreign policy and support for the US Alliance, only the Australian Greens provide an alternative voice. There is, however, growing dialogue and opinions amongst academic and business groups for Australia to take a more independent stance from America on foreign policy in our region. The key dilemma for business and the national economy is Australian trade with China.

Public support for the AAA is still strong, based on a public perception of a security vulnerability long fostered by the ruling political parties.

The signing of the agreement to host US Marines in Darwin was part of Obama's Pacific Pivot. This in turn has led to a new arms race in the region at great financial cost to the people.

In Australia we now have a projected spending of $200 billon on military hardware while many question its value for defending Australia. Included in this are the Joint Strike Fighter (JSF) program and twelve submarines not operational for many years and most likely obsolete by this time.

Global defence contractors are among the largest beneficiaries of Australian government spending. All the big names of military hardware operate here: from Boeing and Raytheon to Lockheed Martin and BAE. Do they donate to political parties? Do they pay much tax in return for billions in taxpayer contracts, contracts that are rarely subject to public scrutiny? Well NO!

Eliot Barham and Michael West crunch the major numbers and take a look at the biggest of them all, BAE Systems. ((*https://www.michaelwest.com. au/defence-giants-the-valley-of-death-is-really-a-mountain-of-money/*)

As well as this planned spending, the government has a policy of promoting manufacturing of military equipment for export with a stated ambition to be one of the top ten exporters internationally. This has led to outrage among many in the community. IPAN is currently working on developing a national campaign of awareness-raising and policy change in relation to military spending.

Along with the financial burden, the military build up has raised the potential for incidents both accidental and planned to spark dangerous confrontations that could lead to major powers at war.

New trends in arms spending are heightening mutual distrust about the intentions and power ambitions of neighbouring states. This distrust is intensified by a lack of effective arms control and transparency mechanisms. There is no regional agreement on arms control, and numerous states in the region have repeatedly circumvented international agreements such as the UN Register of Conventional Arms or the Arms Trade Treaty. The enhancement of available weapon systems makes the potential outcomes of military conflict more severe. Many of the weapons recently acquired are, simply put, more potent and deadly.

Indonesia is a huge archipelago, the most populous predominantly Muslim country in the world, and the most consequential nation in South-east Asia. Indonesia may have a relatively low public profile, but not as far as the Pentagon is concerned – and something important is happening when it comes to US defense and security ties with Jakarta.

For the United States, China's ambitions in the South China Sea constitute a direct challenge to the long-established American military presence in the region. As the world's established superpower faces off against Asia's rising and rival superpower, the stakes could hardly be higher. If the United States is to maintain its maritime position in the face of China's fierce ambitions and rapidly growing capabilities, it will almost certainly require active support from Indonesia

Indonesia has its own colonial history well known in East Timor and in West Papua. China, the US and Australia have increased their military presence in the region with Indonesia resisting falling wholly into line with any. There is pressure on Indonesia from many of the Pacific states to change its policies on West Papua.

Just this month, Australia and Popua New Guinea (PNG) signed an agreement to host a joint naval base on Manus Island, and Australian soldiers could soon begin regular military rotations to PNG as anxiety over China's growing influence in the Pacific region continues to rise.

The Lombrum Naval Base on Manus Island was until recently the facility used to house refugees as part of the Australian off-shore detention system. The Australian Defence Force ran the naval base for twenty-five years until PNG gained independence in 1975. It would be capable of hosting Australian and American warships.

For the peace movement in Australia, most issues of concern revolve around the Alliance with the US, which leads us into wars, unwarranted military spending and allowing our country to be used as a base for power and engaging in future wars.

IPAN is working with a broad section of the community with campaigns on these issues and will address them at the next national conference in Darwin in August 2019.

We intend to host speakers from countries in the SEA and Pacific region.

Your participation and support would be welcome.

Hirohi Inaba
Director, Okinawa Peace Support
Japan

Okinawa is in a dire situation and needs urgent attention from the world now.

The central government is forcibly starting the landfill work at the Oura Bay construction site in the middle of December. In the gubernatorial election held in September, Denny Tamaki won a landslide victory pledging to oppose the new base in Henoko.

Nevertheless, the Abe administration would not give the slightest consideration to halt the construction, deliberately ignoring the collective will of Okinawans. It would not be overstating it to say the Abe administration is like a dictatorship that blatantly denies democracy.

During World War II, Okinawa was the only place in Japan that experienced on-the-ground battle, which took the lives of a quarter of the entire population. It is no wonder that a majority of Okinawans oppose the latest additional US base to be constructed on Okinawa. They are totally justified.

Oura Bay, the intended site of the US military base, has internationally recognized biodiversity, and is home to over 5,400 kinds of marine life, including 262 endangered species. We must not allow the transformation of this pristine and valuable sea into a military base.

Whereas Okinawa's landmass is only 0.6% of the whole of Japan, the percentage of US military bases on Okinawa is 70% of the total throughout Japan. Thus, the historically heavy presence of US military bases has victimized Okinawans with noise pollution from military aircraft, as well as crimes or military accidents caused by US Marines, including robbery, murder, and rape among others.

In the winter of 2016, military aircraft parts fell on the roof of a nursery school and the playground of an elementary school. Just today, we Okinawans were shocked by a report revealing that severe soil contamination by perfluoroctanesulfonic acid (PFOS) and perfluorooctanoic acid (PFOA), typically used in fire-fighting foam, was found at test sites near US bases.

Please stand up for Okinawa! When peace prevails in Okinawa, it will go beyond — to East Asia and to the entire world.

Today, I was truly encouraged by reports given by activists engaging in anti-base movements around the world. It is critical for us to be united.

Let me express my heartfelt gratitude to all.

Okinawa will never give up. We will not fail to stop the new base.

Let's keep fighting together!

Tarak Kauff
Veterans For peace
USA

I want to appreciate what our sister, Dr. Aleida Guevara, said about Indian indigenous wisdom leading this struggle. I think that is very important.

All the organizations gathered here will not lead the revolution that must take place if we are to survive the dual threat of nuclear war and catastrophic climate change. We are here representing and in solidarity with people all over the world who are struggling to survive, to eat, to be free from war and free from occupation.

The indigenous Okinawan resistance to US bases, South Korea's Candlelight Revolution, Jeju Island resistance in South Korea, Native American-led Standing Rock resistance in the US, Palestinian resistance, and the Black Lives Matter resistance in the US will lead the way.

The distance between Okinawa and China is only 500 miles. Seventy-three years ago the people of Okinawa were sacrificed by the Japanese during WWII in the battle of Okinawa, one of the most horrific of the war. Some 150,000 Okinawans perished. They do not want to be a target again. The struggle in Okinawa to prevent the building of a new Marine airbase on pristine Oura Bay has persisted for some fourteen years and despite the combined force of the Japanese government and the US military, the people and the Okinawan governor will not give up.

What is the Asia Pivot? More importantly, what is it not? The Asia Pivot policy has nothing to do with democracy, freedom or security, as US propaganda would claim. It is directly counter to those concerns.

The simple answer is that it is the usual racket. Big bucks for the Air Force and Navy in terms of missile defense, aircraft carriers, both kinds of submarines, fighter jets and new bombers — so that translates into profits for big weapons manufacturers like Boeing, Lockheed Martin, General Dynamics. But it is not just about money. Many people in Washington view American hegemony and dominance as much more important than money.

From the beginning it was, among other things, an effort to develop an operational doctrine for a possible military confrontation with China. This strategic chess game played by the US military/industrial complex can have real-life disastrous consequences.

The signal received in Beijing was the United States had hostile intentions toward China and was trying to contain it militarily. The entire pivot is seen by Beijing as part of an effort to encircle China — which it is.

Missile defense — Terminal High Altitude Area Defense (THAAD) — (really offense) is a key part of US encirclement of China — and Russia. THAAD is essentially part of a first-strike strategy. Missile defense systems have also proven to be capable anti-satellite weapons and are ultimately driving a new arms race with Russia and China.

The Pentagon is now encircling Russia and China with missile defense systems. Why Russia? Russia has the world's largest supply of natural gas and significant supplies of oil.

Why China? The US knows it can't compete with China economically. But China imports 80 percent of its oil on ships. If the Pentagon can choke off China's ability to transport these vital resources then the US would hold the keys to China's economic engine.

Anticipating a future challenge from China in the Asia-Pacific region, the Pentagon launched a new military doctrine called AirSea Battle (ASB) that became official Pentagon policy in 2010. ASB was intended to create a unified war plan that would help the Navy and the Air Force dominate the "battle space" of a war in an environment like the Pacific against an enemy like China.

ASB calls for an integration of Navy and Air Force capabilities that emphasizes highly coordinated "joint operations"—"to guarantee freedom of access, anywhere and in any domain (land, air, space, sea and cyber) for the armed forces of the United States and its allies." Part of what is referred to as full-spectrum dominance. These are deadly games played by highly intelligent people with, unfortunately, a misguided sense of reality.

China's People's Daily newspaper noted, "If the US takes the ASB system seriously, China has to upgrade its anti-access capabilities. China should have the ability to deter any external interference but unfortunately, such a reasonable stance is seen as a threat by the US."

So the dangerous and unnecessary games of war and militarism continue.

In 2012, the US began transferring more troops and weapons to the Korean Peninsula.

The Obama administration's 2012 Pivot to East Asia regional strategy forged a broad-based military presence; while allegedly "advancing democracy and human rights." The perception from China is, correctly, that all of these are part of the US' China containment policy. Proponents of this theory claim that the United States needs a weak, divided China to continue its hegemony in Asia.

Former Chinese State Councilor Dai Bingguo suggested to Hillary Clinton: "Why don't you 'pivot out of here?'"

So that's the Asia Pivot in a nutshell. Our job as human rights and anti-war activists is to be in solidarity, in person where possible, as four veterans delegations to Okinawa and others to South Korea and Palestine were, wherever courageous people are standing up and fighting for their rights and for the planet.

Plenary 5:

The Middle East: US/NATO Plan

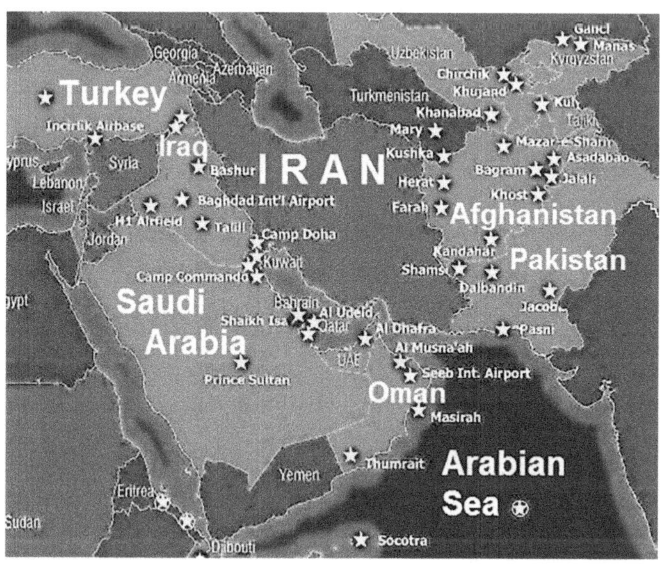

Chair:
MK Aida Touma-Sliman
Peace and Solidarity Committee
Israel

Chair's Opening Remarks

MK Aida Touma-Sliman
Member of Israeli Knesset
President, Peace and Solidarity Committee
Israel

Good afternoon. I am a Palestinian member of the Israeli Knesset.

Allow me firstly to thank the organizers for inviting us — and indeed pushing us — to understand that it was time to hold this kind of international conference that will hopefully lead — and I hope it will lead — to a more enthusiastic campaign all over the world against US and NATO military bases, and any kind of militarization and wars that are being led by those armies and countries that, most of the time, host these bases and that believe that hosting a base is not being a partner in launching a war. When you are hosting a base in your country, any government accepting that is a partner in the crimes that are committed in the wars that are taking place around the world. They should be held responsible for that.

When I was thinking about how to start the discussion in this panel — I am not a speaker on this panel, I am chairing it — I checked on the Internet to see what kind of US military bases operate in Israel. This is a subject that is not discussed in Israel. The cynical thing is that officially the first US military base in Israel was established in 2017. Only last year. How come this was the first time the US officially established a military base in Israel? For me it was always understood that Israel looks like a big US military base in the Middle East. Maybe that is why they do not have to officially establish anything. It is there is the co-operation that is so good the US doesn't have to plant a flag in order to make it clear. Everyone understands that.

The other thing is that they think that they are deceiving the Arab world in that if they establish a military base in Israel the Arab world will be angry. But the Arab world also has US military bases; one of the largest is in Qatar. There are also US military bases in Kuwait and the United Arab Emirates. Around ten Arab countries play host to US military bases. When US aircraft take off from these bases do the people of those countries ask themselves what kind of crimes are being committed against neighbouring Arab countries that are supposed to be their brothers and sisters, that are part of the Arab world as a whole? Of course the rulers of those countries, and those who are benefiting from the bases, do not ask themselves this question. Maybe because the bases are protecting their rule in their countries, where they are oppressing their own people, and because they want to protect themselves more than anything else.

Saying that, I have to add that the Middle East is of interest to the entire world but especially to the US. We usually say that Israel is the back yard — but these days it looks like the front yard — of the United States. It serves as a good American policeman in this region.

During my flight between Istanbul and Dublin, the Israeli Minister of Defence, Avigdor Lieberman, the Minister of War, resigned from the Israeli Government because he could not launch the war that he wanted to launch, because he was not authorised, as he put it, to launch a war against our people, the Palestinian people of Gaza. What is even more painful, however, is that there are now demonstrations taking place in Israel not against the war, not demanding a political agreement to end the occupation of Palestinian lands but to start a war. "Smash them". We are in real danger with this mentality especially as Israel is the only nuclear power in the Middle East. Whoever is claiming there might be a nuclear arms race in the Middle East should, first and foremost, blame the Israeli Government for deciding to have that kind of weapon in Israel.

I would like to introduce our first speaker, Medea Benjamin. There is no way to introduce her other than to describe her as a real fighter for justice, the anti-war movement and peace. Medea is from the US. I have learned a lot from Medea about what she has already achieved in her young life. Medea is an author, and helped organize the freedom march to Gaza, in 2018. She has opposed other conflicts, including the Iraq War, but today she will help us to understand the situation in the Middle East.

Medea Benjamin
Co-Founder, CODEPINK
USA

The Middle East is choc full of US military bases. Sometimes these are in countries whose repressive governments want to host the bases and sometimes they are in countries where the governments have been strong-armed by the United States to be hosts. The countries include Egypt, Qatar, Bahrain, Saudi Arabia, Jordan, Israel, Syria, Turkey, Iraq, Oman, and the United Arab Emirates. In Iraq, after the US invasion in 2003, there was talk about having permanent US bases there. But that is something that must be authorized by Congress, so the Bush administration invented a new term and called them "enduring bases."

And let's not leave out the US military base in Djibouti, right across the Bab el-Mandeb Strait in the horn of Africa. Djibouti is this tiny sliver of land with less than one million people. It not only has a US base where American drones are launched, but it also houses China's first foreign base and Japan's first foreign base. It was a French colony so France has a base there, Italy has a base there, and now the government is in discussions with Russia and Turkey to set up bases. Renting itself out to international militaries is big business for this very repressive government, but one-quarter of the local people still live in absolute poverty.

In addition to these bases throughout the region, there are also "floating bases" all over Middle East waters. There are about 16,000 US personnel at sea and more than 40 US Navy ships that belong to the US Fifth Fleet.

And then there are covert bases for covert operations that none of us, even the US taxpayers who pay for all this, are allowed to know about.

Why does the US have all these bases? One reason is because this region is so rich in oil, gas and other resources. Other reasons include protecting Israel, shoring up repressive governments that the US wants to support, and confronting Iran.

There are two particularly enormous bases. One is in Bahrain, where the Fifth Fleet is based. It is also the place where there was a beautiful democratic uprising in 2011 as part of the Arab Spring. The Saudis rolled into the country on US tanks and crushed this nonviolent, inspiring uprising. To this day, the US is supporting the very repressive government of Bahrain that has brutally cracked down on all forms of dissent.

The other enormous base is in Qatar. It is an airbase with about 10,000 US personnel, It is the nerve center of US air campaigns in the region, including dropping bombs in Iraq, Afghanistan and Syria, According to the US government website, every ten minutes there are aircraft coming in or taking off from Qatar.

Saudi Arabia recently initiated a campaign to boycott Qatar because it has a decent relationship with Saudi's nemesis, Iran. The Saudis cut off relations and imposed a blockade on Qatar. Donald Trump, who loves Saudi Arabia, seems to have said, "Oh go ahead and attack Qatar, that's fine," until someone must have tapped him on the shoulder and pointed out that since the US has its largest base in the Middle East in Qatar, maybe it would be better not to take sides.

The US has been taking sides — the side of Saudi Arabia — ever since massive oil reserves were discovered there in 1938. And it's not just the United States. It is the entire western world. The great western democracies have supported this repressive government since the time of its founding. They have ignored the internal repression — against women, against the Shia minority, against the ten million foreign workers, many of whom are treated like indentured servants. Saudi Arabia is also a country that doesn't even pretend to have elections, a country where there is no freedom of speech, freedom of the press, freedom of assembly. And then we have the horrific case of the Saudi journalist, Jamal Khashoggi, who was murdered and chopped up in the Saudi consulate in Turkey for writing articles critical of the megalomaniac crown prince Mohammad bin Salman. This has created a bit of a dilemma for the Western world about how to keep justifying its relationship with Saudi Arabia.

Since we are talking about military bases here, it is important to note that the US bases in Saudi Arabia were the catalyst for Osama bin Laden to declare war against the United States. The Saudi rulers allowed the US, under President George Bush Sr., to bring in hundreds of thousands of US troops to the Kingdom during the Gulf War in 1991. Bin Laden said this was a tremendous humiliation for the Saudi people and said it marked a turning point in his life. Later on, after the 9/11 attacks, George Bush Jr. quietly closed those bases in Saudi Arabia but they were re-opened by President Obama.

I talked about internal repression in Saudi Arabia, but must also acknowledge that the Saudis are involved in a brutal war in neighboring Yemen, with a bombing campaign so severe that it has destroyed that nation's infrastructure and created a catastrophic situation of hunger and disease. Again, we see the US and Western countries aligning with the Saudis by selling them the very weapons used to murder Yemeni civilians. We must all work harder to stop our countries from selling weapons to the Saudis.

It is very hard to stop wars once they start, which is why it is so important to do all we can to stop wars BEFORE they start. And in this sense it's important to talk about Iran, where the US is setting the stage for another war.

The Trump administration pulled out of the Iran nuclear deal, a deal that is working and stops Iran from getting nuclear weapons. Let's be clear: Iran has zero nuclear weapons. Israel has hundreds and will not allow any inspectors in or join any international treaty on nuclear weapons. And the US has thousands of nuclear weapons. You can imagine what it is like from the Iranian point of view to see this hypocrisy. We don't want ANY country to have nuclear weapons, and that includes our own countries.

Nevertheless, Donald Trump called the Iran nuclear agreement a "terrible deal." He withdrew from the agreement and reinstated crippling sanctions that are keeping even needed medicines from the people. The European Union and other nations are trying to circumvent these sanctions, but with the power of the almighty dollar, it is not clear whether they can succeed.

And while the US accuses Iran of "meddling" in the region, the very region where it resides, the US has been building up military bases all around Iran. There is a political cartoon that shows Iran literally surrounded by US bases, with a caption saying, "Iran Wants War: Look How Close they Put Their Country to Our Military Bases."

Our job is to work together to try to stop a war with Iran, and we thank our European allies for standing up against the Trump administration's bellicose policy on Iran.

Thank you for your time and efforts. I look forward to working more closely together to close foreign military bases and end all wars.

Richard Boyd Barrett, TD
Member of Dail Eireann [Irish Parliament]
Ireland

I would like to thank Peace and Neutrality Alliance (PANA) and the other organizers for inviting me to speak at this conference.

Earlier today, I attending a housing protest — we are currently experiencing a housing crisis in Ireland. I mentioned to a young protestor that I was coming to this conference to speak about Palestine. The young protestor asked me how the world could permit what is happening in Palestine. Month after month, year after year, decade after decade, the people of Palestine have been subjected to unrelenting horrific treatment, which continues, including murder, imprisonment, the demolition of houses, land seizures and military assault, in a naked demonstration of racism by Israel, as has been brutally and openly expressed in their new nation-state law. There is no pretence of anything else in that law not that there was ever very much pretence about their actions on the part of the State of Israel. All this is happening right in front of us but the world stands idly by watching the annexation of territory in breach of the Oslo Accords. Gaza is being subject to a relentless siege and is being strangled without clean water, and without access to sewage and sanitation.

Why is this happening?

What is happening in Palestine gives the lie to any notion that the European Union and the United States are champions of democracy. The treatment of Palestine has been part of the West's strategy since the early 20th century to control the oil-rich Middle East. We in Ireland are familiar with this. Sir Ronald Stokes, a British official in Palestine, said in 1936 that Britain's plan was to create "a loyal little Jewish Ulster" in the Middle East to guard against a potentially hostile sea of Arabism. Stokes and Arthur Balfour, who, as British Foreign Secretary in 1917 issued the famous Balfour Declaration promising the Jews a homeland in Palestine, had been architects of British oppression in Ireland: Balfour as Prime Minister from 1902 to 1905 and later as British Foreign Secretary and Stokes as a British official who oversaw the activities of the notorious Black and Tans and Auxiliaries, thugs recruited by the British Government during the Irish War of Independence.

The West's strategy has been to divide and conquer, for centuries a British imperial tactic. The strategy was to divide the Middle East against itself and to create a military encampment in Israel, which acts as the West's watchdog. Apartheid is in the very DNA of the State of Israel. Those of us who say that are accused of being anti-Semitic but the exact opposite is the truth. It is because we are horrified by the Nazi Holocaust against the Jews that we now oppose a political project — Zionism — that is racist in its very essence.

How should the world respond to the State of Israel?

The State of Israel must be dismantled. We must support the boycott and divestment campaigns. We must treat Israel the way we treated apartheid South Africa. Israel has no interest in a two-state solution. If they did, they would not have broken the Oslo Accords, indeed hours after signing it! In any event, it is not possible to compromise with Israel any more than it was with apartheid S. Africa although some people favoured such an accommodation. That was not acceptable, however, and we can say the same about Israel. The Zionist project must be dismantled.

Despite the cynical support for Israel on the part of the West, I am hopeful about the future. We are starting to win hearts and minds across the world. The Great March for Return, a six week campaign of protests launched by Palestinians in the Gaza Strip on 30 March 2018 calling for Palestinian refugees' right of return to their homes and villages in today's Israel from which they were driven out in 1948, undermines any attempt to portray the Palestinians as terrorists. We should support any further marches for return by organizing demonstrations on a global basis similar to those against the Iraq war in 2003.

Dr. Asad Abushark
Spokeperson, Great March of Return
Palestine

Thank you very much everybody.

I would like to thank you for inviting me and for giving me the opportunity of speaking to you today. I would also like to convey warm greetings from the Palestinian people and especially from the Great March of Return in Gaza to you and to ask for your support and help for the Palestinian people. It is now high time to support the Palestinian people.

We have been discussing US and NATO bases throughout the world but we have forgotten one: the most dangerous, the most threatening, American-protected, American-armed, NATO-supported, NATO-supplied military base in the world. It is, in the words of Noam Chomsky, the rogue State of Israel, apartheid Israel, which practices racism against the Palestinian people.

But who created the State of Israel and when? I'll take you back to the year 1917, the 2nd November, to the Balfour Declaration. Arthur Balfour was the British Foreign Minister at that time. In the words of the writer, Arthur Koestler, in the Balfour Declaration "one nation promised another nation the country of a third nation." So my country was given to my enemies to live there. They supported them. They armed them. Following the Balfour Declaration and the subsequent handing over of Palestine to Britain under the Mandate, Herbert Samuel, who was a Zionist, was appointed the first British High Commissioner to facilitate the immigration, arming and supporting of Zionist Jews from all over the world. This is what happened until 1948 when we were ethnically cleansed. The majority of the Palestinian people, around one million strong, became refugees. I am one of them, as is my son, who is here, who is still a refugee also. I was a refugee as a baby, as a boy, as a teenager, as a young man, as an old man and will probably also be as a dead man. This is why I want you to understand the catastrophe of the Palestinian people, which has been described by Professor Illan Pappe, an Israeli historian, as ethnic cleansing.

How did they manage this? The British were of course responsible and then the Americans came to help. But what are the means? Because the Zionist movement is terrorist in its goal, in its objectives and in practice. According to Professor Baruch Kimmerling, an Israeli sociologist, Israel will use the following crimes to wipe out, to exterminate, to annihilate the Palestinian people:

1. Genocide — to kill the whole Palestinian people
2. Ethnocide — to get rid of the Palestinian race
3. Sociocide — to destroy Palestinian society
4. Politicide — to destroy the political parties and institutions of the Palestinian people
5. Urbicid — to destroy the infrastructure, the towns and cities of Palestinian society, and to establish Israeli towns and cities with Hebrew names to facilitate the fifth objective,
6. Memorycide — to brainwash and manipulate the minds of the world.

The American administration is complicit in what has happened since 1948. From Truman to Trump they have all supported Israel. Just fifteen minutes after the proclamation of the State of Israel President Truman said "Israel is there to stay". His successors have also supported Israel. President Nixon said that Israel is paying for American security with the only cost to the US being an aircraft carrier in the Mediterranean Sea. President GWH Bush said that the US has an unbreakable bond with Israel with whom the US shares Judeo-Christian values. He said that Israel is an asset to US security, an integral part of US security. President Obama spoke of the unbreakable bond between the US and Israel and gave Israel $38 billion dollars in military, material and moral support. President Clinton did the same. Madeline Albright, on a visit to Gaza with President Clinton, said that "we [the US] will maintain Israel's qualitative military supremacy in the Middle East". Henceforth, Israel is being protected militarily and in the United

Nations by the United States. No less than forty seven vetoes have been exercised by the US on Israel's behalf at the United Nations.

Many resolutions have been adopted by the United Nations in favour of the Palestinian people. I will remind you of some of them. Resolution 194, which calls for our right of return. That is why the marchers for return in Gaza carry this slogan: to remind the world of the UN Resolution, which calls for the return of the Palestinian people and for compensation for those who were driven out of their homes by the Zionist gang in 1948. And Resolution 3236 (1975), which calls for the inalienable rights of the Palestinian people. What are these rights?

1. The right of return of, and compensation for, all Palestinian refugees to their homes and property from which they were evicted by Israel in 1948.
2. The right to self-determination.
3. The right to statehood and sovereignty.
4. The right to use all legitimate means, including armed struggle, to liberate their land.

Unfortunately, the United States is standing against the Palestinian people. As is NATO. As is the Quartet. The Palestinian people believe there is an international conspiracy of silence. Many countries are complicit in the crime of ethnic cleansing and annihilation of the Palestinian people. This is why the Palestinian people launched the Boycott, Divestment and Sanctions (BDS) Movement, which is very important. This is why we call on the whole world to boycott Israel, to divest your investments from Israel and to impose sanctions on Israel because of their crimes against the Palestinian people. Each crime is a crime against humanity, against mankind, against your fellow human beings in Gaza. To add more crimes, Israel imposed a brutal siege on Gaza. I come from there. Over the last ten years Israel launched three genocidal wars against Gaza. The situation in Gaza can be described in two words: life and death and death and life. Gaza is a land of waste or in the words of the British poet, T.S. Elliot, a waste land. That is the situation in Gaza. Hospitals do not have enough drugs. Water is polluted. Infrastructure has been destroyed, including my home and the homes of many other Palestinian people in Gaza. That is why I came to Ireland.

I have been a refugee many times. Unfortunately, there are many refugees like me. The State of Israel is terrorist in goal, in theory and in practice. Israeli

Prime Minister Netanyahu was asked the other day what he would give the Palestinians. He said and I quote "something less than a state but more than self-rule", a bastardized thing in international relations. What is that? He said Israel will never, ever allow the Palestinian refugees to return. He was echoing David Ben-Gurion, who said many years ago, in 1937, that there is nothing immoral in driving the Palestinians out of Palestine. Menachem Begin said that without the massacre of Deir Yassin in 1948 there would not have been a State of Israel.

And they call us all sorts of things. Menachem Begin said that the Palestinians were animals walking on two feet. A former Chief Rabbi of Israel said that the Palestinians are serpents and a former Israeli chief-of-staff, Rafael Eitan, said that the Palestinians are no more than dead, rotten cockroaches in a closed bottle. A former Chairman of the Knesset's Foreign Relations Committee said that Palestine does not belong to the Palestinian Arabs even if they live there and it belongs to the Jews even if they don't live there.

Israel is racist. More dangerous than apartheid South Africa. It practices what apartheid South Africa used to practice. Israel is practising torture. Thousands of Palestinians are in prison. Gaza is under siege. Two million people in Gaza live in miserable conditions. How can this happen in the 21st century? What would the world's reaction be if this was happening to a European country, if there was an earthquake or a tsunami there? The whole word would rush to help. But in the case of the Palestinians, who are being suffocated and killed, who live under a brutal medieval regime, nobody cares. Nobody raises a finger. The nation state law of Israel, which was recently enacted by the Knesset, states that Israel is a Jewish State and is the property of the Jews and only Jews. The Palestinians who live in Israel are merely residents, have no rights, no equal status and their language is not considered to be an official language of the state.

Richard Falk, the United Nations Human Rights Rapporteur for Palestine, has said that Israel is committing the following crimes:

1. Dispossession — dispossessing the Palestinian people of their land, their money, their future
2. Fragmentation — the fragmentation of Palestinian society (West Bank, Gaza, Jerusalem), treating each category separately
3. Misuse of hard power — using lethal weapons to kill as many Palestinians as possible
4. Use of soft power, which means launching smear campaigns, defamation and personality assassination as well as dirty propaganda, and

focusing on its psychological warfare with Iran.

As I said earlier, the United States vetoes all UN resolutions in favour of the Palestinian people, for example, UN Resolution No. 194 of 1948, which calls for the right of return of, and compensation for, all Palestinian refugees driven out by Zionist ethnic cleansing, which we call Nakba; Resolution 3236 of 1975, which calls for the implementation of the inalienable national rights of the Palestinian people, including the right of return and the right of self-determination and statehood; and Resolution 2334 of 2017, which condemns Israel's racism and racist laws and which calls for the dismantling of Israeli settlements on Palestinian lands. The US also opposed the international advisory opinion of the International Court of Justice in The Hague against the apartheid wall, which Israel built to annex more Palestinian land. As I also said above, the US has, to date, used its veto in the United Nations Security Council against the Palestinian people and in favour of Israel no less than forty seven times. This encourages Israel to continue its policy of ethnic cleansing, including the expropriation of Palestinian land, the building of more colonies and settlements on lands grabbed from their Palestinian owners, the enlarging of existing colonial settlements, the tightening of its control of Jerusalem and the maximizing of the land of Israel while minimising the number of Palestinian Arabs. In doing so, Israel is ignoring all UN resolutions breaching the human rights of the Palestinian people, is launching more genocidal wars against the Palestinian people and is engaging in aggression against neighbouring Arab states, including Syria and Lebanon.

Apartheid Israel is co-operating with and supporting the most dictatorial and despotic regimes and military dictatorships in the world. One of the most obnoxious, notorious and nefarious crimes committed by apartheid Israel, and encouraged by the Trump administration and his likes, is the medieval, brutal, excruciating and ever tightening hermitic siege on the Gaza Strip, which has been described by human rights activists such as Richard Falk, Noam Chomsky and Illan Pappe as an open air prison, a slow death concentration camp and the biggest prison on earth.

The US imposed itself as an honest broker for peace. What peace? Pax Americana. Pax Israelita. The US is the most dishonest peace broker. They keep paying lip service to peace. They introduced the so-called road map, which is road-less and map-less. The US is only interested in making Israel its most deterring military base in the Middle East well equipped with hundreds of nuclear weapons and US-supplied technology. This is the double standard policy or the policy of war of mass deception. The famous British historian, Arnold Toynbee, said that if the US applied a fair-handed policy in the Middle East the Palestinian people could not have been evicted from their homeland.

The Palestinian people, who are fighting for a just cause, to liberate their country from the most sophisticated Western and Zionist military base in the Middle East, that is to say, the settler, Zionist, colonial state of Israel, which is based on elimination and dehumanisation, to quote Illan Pappe, call upon the peace-loving and freedom-loving people of the world to support our struggle

— by being an integral part of the international BDS campaign

— by imposing an arms embargo on apartheid Israel,

— by escalating the international solidarity campaign of the Palestinian people by supporting the Great March of Return and by dismantling the racist, Zionist State of Israel and establishing, in its place, a democratic Palestine for all its citizens regardless of religion or ethnicity,

— by supporting the Palestinian struggle morally, materially and with all possible means, including international law, human rights law, including the Fourth Geneva Convention, the Universal Declaration of Human Rights, the UN Charter and all other UN resolutions in favour of the Palestinian cause.

Your solidarity is of paramount importance, which, coupled with the Palestinian people, will lead to the dismantling of the settler, colonial State of Israel as an imperialist US and NATO military base. When that happens, a new dawn will emerge for a free, democratic Palestine where all will live in justice, equality, freedom, dignity and peace.

The struggle continues. We will win. We will not be overcome.

Thank you very much.

Plenary 6:

Europe / Expansion of NATO

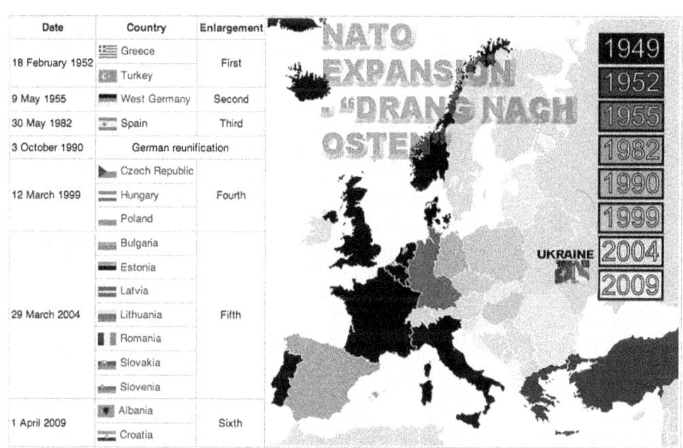

Date	Country	Enlargement
18 February 1952	Greece	First
	Turkey	
9 May 1955	West Germany	Second
30 May 1982	Spain	Third
3 October 1990	German reunification	
12 March 1999	Czech Republic	Fourth
	Hungary	
	Poland	
29 March 2004	Bulgaria	Fifth
	Estonia	
	Latvia	
	Lithuania	
	Romania	
	Slovakia	
	Slovenia	
1 April 2009	Albania	Sixth
	Croatia	

Chair:
David Swanson
World BEYOND War
USA

Chair's Opening Remarks

David Swanson
Director, World BEYOND War
USA

I'm willing to bet that if I asked everyone in Ireland whether the Irish government should take orders from Donald Trump, most people would say no. But last year the Irish Ambassador to the United States came to the University of Virginia, and I asked her how allowing US troops to use Shannon Airport to get to their wars could possibly be in compliance with Irish neutrality. She replied that the US government "at the highest level" had assured her it was all perfectly legal. And she apparently bowed and obeyed. But I don't think the people of Ireland are as inclined to sit and roll over on command as their ambassador.

— Collaboration in crimes is not legal.
— Bombing people's houses is not legal.
— Threatening new wars is not legal.
— Keeping nuclear weapons in other people's countries is not legal.
— Propping up dictators, organizing assassins, murdering people with robotic airplanes: none of it is legal.
— US military bases around the world are the local franchises of the greatest criminal enterprise on earth!

***

And NATO involvement doesn't make a crime any more legal or acceptable.

A lot of people in the United States have trouble distinguishing NATO from the United Nations. And they imagine both of them as murder-laundering operations — that is, as entities that can render mass murder legal, proper, and humanitarian. A lot of people think the US Congress possesses this same magical ability. A presidential war is an outrage, but a Congressional war is enlightened philanthropy. And yet, I have not found a single person in Washington, D.C. — and I've asked Senators and street vendors — not a single person who tells me they would give the slightest damn if Washington was being bombed whether it was being bombed at the order of a parliament, a president, the United Nations, or NATO. The view is always different from under the bombs.

The US military and its European accomplices make up some three quarters of the world's militarism in terms of their own investment in wars plus their dealing of weapons to others. Attempts to claim that an external threat exists have reached ludicrous levels. I can't imagine weapons companies would like anything more than some intra-NATO competition. We need to tell advocates of a European military that you can't oppose US madness by imitating it. If you don't want to buy more weapons on Trump's orders, the answer is not to run off and buy even more under another name. This is a vision of a future dedicated to high tech barbarism, and we don't have time for it.

We don't have the years left to be monkeying around with medieval balances of power. This planet is doomed as a habitable place for us, and the hell that is to come can be lessened only by outgrowing the acceptance of war.

The answer to Trump is not to outdo him but to do the opposite of him.

A tiny fraction of what just the United States spends just on foreign bases could end starvation, the lack of clean water, and various diseases. Instead we get these bases, these toxic instigators of war encircled by zones of drunkenness, rape, and cancer-causing chemicals.

War and preparations for war are the top destroyers of our natural environment.

They are a top cause of death and injury and destruction.

— War is the top source of the erosion of liberties.
— The top justification for government secrecy.
— The top creator of refugees.
— The top saboteur of the rule of law.
— The top facilitator of xenophobia and bigotry.
— The top reason we are at risk of nuclear apocalypse.
— War is not necessary, not just, not survivable, not glorious.
— We need to leave the entire institution of war behind us.
— We need to create a world beyond war.

People have signed the declaration of peace at worldbeyondwar.org in more countries than the United States has troops in.

People's movements are on our side. Justice is on our side. Sanity is on our side. Love is on our side.

We are many. They are few.

No to NATO. No to bases. No to wars in distant places.

Ilda Figueiredo
Chairperson, CPPC
Portugal

Dear Friends

On behalf of the Portuguese Council for Peace and Cooperation (CPPC) I salute this important meeting, our host Peace and Neutrality Alliance (PANA), and everybody who is participating here.

As we said in our report about Europe, the step up of US militarism has been particularly visible and worrying in Europe, with the sending of more troops and military equipment, with the warmongering actions of NATO and its continuing enlargement — aimed at the Russian Federation. A step up that is part of the general escalation in military aggressiveness and destabilization operations by the US and its allies, be it in the Middle East, Latin America, the Pacific Region or Africa, be it against Palestine, Syria, Yemen, Iran, Venezuela, Cuba, the Korean Peninsula, or China — among other serious premeditated tension situations.

The USA, NATO and the European Union's great powers and their allies, in their ambition for world domination, are the great threats to peace and the peoples. They are responsible for the exponential increase in military expenditures, the race for new, more sophisticated and destructive weapons — namely nuclear weapons — and the escalation in interference, threats, provocation and destabilization operations, which threaten to unleash conflicts of great and unimaginable consequences for humanity, including with the use of nuclear weapons.

Let us recall that the USA is aiming at a record high military budget of over $700 billion, and that European NATO members have decided to double their military spending by 2024. Let us recall also that USA/NATO/ EU and their main allies are responsible for more than 70% of the total military expenditure in the world.

As was noticeable at the last United Nations General Assembly, the USA and its allies are also responsible for a violent attack on the UN Charter and international law that define important rights of the peoples and principles that should govern international relations, created after the end of World War II, as a result of the correlation of forces that were favourable to peace, national liberation, democracy and social progress.

The EU, as a supra-national political and military structure — dominated by the great powers, especially Germany — continues to foment its policies against the rights and living conditions of workers and peoples, against national sovereignty and independence, trying to impose increasing exploitation and attacking labour and social rights, that are at the origin of the high indexes of job instability, poverty and the degradation of living conditions of millions upon millions of workers, retired people, pensioners, youth, women and children.

With the deepening of the economic and social crisis and the exploitation of the situation of thousands of immigrants — that long for the right to a dignified life — and of thousands of refugees — that flee from the destabilization operations, from the wars of aggression of the US, NATO and the EU and its allies, in several European countries extreme right-wing, xenophobe and fascist forces continue to rise.

With the pretext of "fighting against terrorism", in several countries and at EU level, a "securitarian" drift is taking place attacking freedoms, guarantees and fundamental rights.

In a situation in which there are evident increasing contradictions, the EU continues to work hand in hand with US/NATO. The deepening of European Union militarisation is particularly worrying, with military cooperation through the launch of Permanent Structured Cooperation (PESCO), the creation of a European Defence Fund, the implementation of a European Defence Industrial Program to develop the European weapons industry, or further steps to ensure the funding for the EU's battle groups. This EU step up in militarization, and the creation of the so called "European Army" that — not without rivalries — converges with the US, is leading to the increased militarization of EU as the European pillar of NATO or a complementary part of this political-military bloc.

In parallel and complementary to NATO, EU military structures are developing a French military initiative, the so-called "European Intervention Initiative" (EI2), a joint military structure between nine European countries, including Germany.

Fundamentally, we note the alignment of the EU with the increasing US and NATO interference and the warmongering against the Russian Federation, and also towards other countries from Europe, Africa, the Middle East, Central Asia or even Latin America. The European Union is continuing its policy of collusion with Israel that illegally occupies Palestine and represses the Palestinian people, and with Morocco, which illegally occupies Western Sahara and represses the Sahrawi people.

The strengthening of the struggle against war and militarism, for peace and disarmament and for solidarity with the peoples — victims of interference and aggression of imperialism — presents itself as one of the most urgent tasks of our time.

The struggles of the peace-loving peoples of the world against the brutal imperialist offensive, war and militarisation, in the defence of peoples' rights, the sovereignty and independence of the states, for peace, liberty, democracy, for the right to development, to justice, social progress, for the protection of the environment, human rights and cultural heritage, show that war can, and must be prevented.

Faced with the attack on the UN Charter and on international law it is urgent to defend principles such as the peoples' right to self-determination, national sovereignty and independence, non-interference in the internal affairs of states, the peaceful solution of international conflicts, the end of all forms of oppression, including national oppression, universal, simultaneous and controlled disarmament, the dissolution of political-military blocs, the cooperation among the peoples and countries for a new world order of peace, emancipation and for humanity's progress.

Remembering the example of past struggles, it is fundamental to promote the convergence and unity of all consequent and broad forces for peace and progress in a strong mobilization whose strength, breadth and conviction is needed to prevent new tragedies from occurring.

It is fundamental to building unity in action, based upon our principles, among the broad peace and anti-imperialist forces, to strengthen and develop an effective and broad movement for peace.

We organized some of the joint and converging events and initiatives developed by, or with the significant participation of the World Peace Council's European member organizations as the "Yes to Peace! No to NATO!"

Campaign and actions in Brussels, Belgium, where NATO held its summit on 11-12 July 2018.

In the framework of the WPC's "Yes to Peace! No to NATO!" Campaign, actions against NATO were held by several organizations in their respective countries, as in Portugal.

CPPC has continued to develop with dozens of other Portuguese organizations the campaign Yes to Peace! No to NATO! Promoting debates, public initiatives and demonstrations that involved a multitude of people, the distribution of thousands of leaflets and other documents all around the country, spreading among the people the need to struggle for peace and disarmament, against militarism and war, and consequently the need to fight against NATO and for its dissolution.

With this campaign, the Portuguese people denounce NATO and the warmongering goals of its Brussels summit, denouncing NATO as an instrument aimed at serving — notwithstanding internal quarrels — the political, economic and geostrategic interests of the United States and the great powers of the European Union (EU), an instrument that drives the arms race, promotes areas of tension and conflict, intensifies military interventionism, and carries out wars of aggression against states and peoples, who defend their sovereignty and do not submit to their domination. The evolution of the international situation shows clearly that NATO is at the service of the plans for hegemonic domination of the world by the USA.

The campaign organized several street initiatives in various cities, like Lisbon and Porto.

Adding to the campaign, CPPC has frequently distributed other documents and statements denouncing NATO and its objectives.

CPPC has issued several statements and documents, including posters, denouncing the ongoing deepening of the militarization process of the EU, with steps like the launch of Permanent Structured Cooperation (PESCO), the creation of a European Defence Fund and the implementation of a European Defence Industrial Program for developing the European weapons industry.

Against nuclear weapons, CPPC has promoted several initiatives and statements for the total elimination of nuclear weapons. The initiatives include a campaign for Portugal to sign and ratify the Treaty on the Prohibition of Nuclear Weapons, that contained a petition already delivered to the Portuguese Parliament and that will be discussed at a Plenary Meeting of Parliament, an exhibition that has several copies travelling the country and is being shown in schools, in public spaces and events.

One big Meeting for Peace, promoted by CPPC and eleven organizations and entities, was held on October 20. At this meeting, attended by more than 700 people from around the country, more than fifty organizations participated.

We consider this to have been an important moment in the development of the defence of peace in Portugal. A moment of sharing experiences and views by men and women of all ages, leaders and activists from the organizations involved, union leaders, elected officials, religious people, priests, military personnel, teachers, journalists, researchers, legal experts, and students, among others.

Next year, we will commemorate the seventieth anniversary of the Congrés Mondial des Partisans de la Paix, that was held, in 1949, simultaneously in Paris and Prague. We recall that the Manifesto of that Congress proclaimed the fundamental objectives and principles of our movement, like the defence of the principles of the UN Charter, the banning of nuclear and other weapons of mass extermination, national independence and peaceful cooperation of all peoples, self determination, denouncing all military alliances, the burden of military expenditure and the propaganda that seeks to prepare public opinion for war.

At a time like the one we are living in, marked by mounting tensions and the militarization of international relations; by increasing interference, destabilization and wars of aggression; by the disrespect for the independence of states and the sovereignty and the rights of the peoples; marked by an increase in military expenditure and the arms race — as a result of a warmongering policy promoted by the USA, EU, NATO and their allies — we must keep in mind the example of the defenders of peace that, in equally harsh times, knew, despite differences, how to determine the main threat and danger, uniting forces against a new war and in the defence of peace and the survival of humankind. Let us raise high and pursue today and in the future their legacy and their struggle.

Yes to Peace! No to NATO!

Frank Keoghan
Secretary, People's Movement
Ireland

In 2017, Jean Claude Juncker, European Union (EU) Commission President, proclaimed that: "By 2025 we need a fully-fledged European Defence Union. We need it. And NATO wants it."

Now, Brussels has signalled that military union is the preferred next stage of EU integration. This development is facilitated by the Lisbon Treaty, or EU Constitution, which obliges Member States to support the EU's security policy "actively and unreservedly in a spirit of loyalty and mutual solidarity" (Article 24.3 Treaty on European Union). In 2016 Juncker called for a "security union with the end goal of establishing a European army" while the EU Parliament called for the EU to upgrade its military to be able to use "its full potential as a world power."

The Lisbon Treaty contains a mutual defence clause (Art.42.7 TEU) and a separate obligation to participate in an EU "common defence", - an EU Army. Furthermore, "[t]he common security and defence policy shall include the progressive framing of a common Union defence policy. This will lead to a common defence when the European Council, acting unanimously, so decides." (Art.42.2 TEU).

"Member States shall make civilian and military capabilities available to the Union for the implementation of the common security and defence policy…. Member States shall undertake progressively to improve their military capabilities." This last provision is a commitment to a continual arms build-up amongst EU States — exactly what is envisaged in Permanent Structured Cooperation (PESCO).

The Lisbon Treaty also established the European Defence Agency (EDA), which identifies "operational requirements, promoting measures to satisfy those requirements and … shall participate in defining a European capabilities and armaments policy.…" (Arts.42.3 and 45 TEU). This body is now the focus of continual lobbying by Europe's arms manufacturers, who continually push cross-national integration and a common security and defence agenda.

The European Council decided just months after the Britain's Brexit referendum to increase the emphasis on EU militarisation in response to calls by Germany. Britain had opposed greater EU cooperation on defence, seeing this as the preserve of NATO. Now, the Franco-Germans and the Brussels bureaucracy could press ahead on military matters without Britain restraining them — though nuclear — armed Britain has pledged to continue military cooperation.

The Lisbon Treaty explicitly recognises the NATO alliance as the prime forum for the collective defence of its members and EU military policy as complementary to but separate from NATO's. (Art.42.7 TEU and Protocol No. 10.)

But, "[t]he current level of cooperation between NATO and the EU is unprecedented," according to Elżbieta Bieńkowska, internal market commissioner, while the Conclusions of the Juune 2018 EU Council called for 'further deepening of EU-NATO cooperation.' This was reinforced by NATO Secretary-General Stoltenberg, following the July NATO summit: "We just finished a fruitful meeting on NATO-EU co-operation. Over the past two years, we have achieved unprecedented levels of cooperation and we have been working together in seventy-four concrete areas."

In his "State of the Union" address delivered in September, Mr. Juncker emphasized his demand for the EU to play a united, powerful role in global policy, repeating verbatim formulations used by German politicians to promote a more aggressive German military policy. He called for "Europe to get off the side-lines of world affairs." It should no longer be a "mere commentator on international events." The EU must finally act as a "global player" and take "its destiny into its own hands" and must become an "architect of tomorrow's world."

A primary focus in Mr. Juncker's plans was the EU's militarisation, promising that he would "work day and night," to see the European Defence Fund and PESCO become fully operational. He is also contemplating "to increase defence spending by a factor of 20."

In 2017, the Council of Ministers established PESCO under Arts. 42 and 46 TEU. These commit the participating Member States to "the principle of a single set of forces;" to increasing their military spending to reach specific monitored target levels, and to providing troops for EU combat missions.

At the same time, the EU Commission proposed the establishment of a European Defence Fund, EU defence chief, Federica Mogherini, calling it "a historic day for European defence."

Up to 2020, the defence fund will receive an annual €90 million from the EU's budget — to which Ireland is a net contributor — for military research, and half a billion euro for military development. It is projected that the fund will spend €49bn between 2021 and 2027 on research into new military technologies, such as robotics and cyber defence. The EU Council asked the European Investment Bank to support these projects and the latter has recently changed its rules. Horizon 2020, an €80bn research programme, has also allocated significant funds for military programmes.

In October, German defence minister Ursula von der Leyen, said that the structures for a European Defence Union have been "activated." "The structures that have been 'sleeping' for a long time inside the Treaty of Lisbon; we have activated them. That means we now have a legal framework for a European Defence Union, we have a joint planning process, so that as Europeans we can also develop a structure that tells us when we are going to use our forces."

EU military interventions in Africa, the Balkans and the Middle East are titled "peace-making" or "peace-keeping". Troops wear EU uniforms on these missions. Their actions are supported by the European Defence Agency, the EU Satellite Centre and the EU Military Committee (EUMC). The latter oversees the EU Military Staff (EUMS) headquartered in Brussels.

Simultaneously, the EU Commission is continuing the fortification of the EU's external borders. The European Border and Coast Guard was established in 2016, with a force of 1,500 members. Original proposals estimated that this would increase to 10,000 by 2027; but a recent proposal by Mr. Juncker, accelerates this timetable by seven years. He aims to spend €1.3 billion to add an additional 10,000 border guards by 2020.

The powers of this proposed force are particularly notable. It would operate with executive powers and its own equipment, being deployed "wherever and whenever" along the EU's external borders, as well as in non-EU countries. Its equipment is to include "vessels, planes and vehicles, available to be deployed at all times and for all necessary operations."

It can end its soldiers even if the destination country doesn't want them, and Member-States surrender the legal right to have a monopoly of force within their own borders. For the first time there will be a pan-EU military force with the right to go anywhere it wants within the EU.

There are also eighteen EU Battlegroups, each able to deploy 1,500 men speedily from different member states on a rotating basis. Ireland will participate in a 2019 EU Battlegroup, forming a "significant element" within a German-led battle group on standby.

And will Brexit diminish the effectiveness of an EU Army? Well, the old imperial powers, Germany and Britain, have signed a "joint vision statement." It provides for common steps in training missions outside Europe, in the "fight against terrorism" and in weapons development.

And last month, it was decided that Britain (and the US) will have access to PESCO on a case-by-case basis after Brexit. "The invited third state should provide substantial added value to achieving the objectives of the individual project (contributing with resources or expertise)," creating a permanent link between Brexit Britain and the EU Army.

A review by the Bundestag earlier this year determined that Germany could legally finance French or British nuclear weapons on German soil in exchange for their protection. The EU could do the same, if it changed its budgetary rules.

Germany could be granted shared control over the use of warheads under a "dual-key" system and German ruling circles have renewed a debate about "going nuclear." A "Euro-bomb" with a German finger on an EU nuclear trigger would be an important step on that road.

Meanwhile, France is planning a €37 billion seven - year revamp of its nuclear arsenal and it seems increasingly likely that they will be able to provide an EU nuclear capability. Upgrades to France's land-based and sea-based nuclear deterrent will be part of the astonishing €300 billion to be spent by 2025. German bases and German financing would enable it to pose as a guarantor of EU security.

NATO's 2018 Summit Declaration characterises the EU as a "unique and essential partner for NATO," and speaks of a "strategic partnership" between the two organisations while agreeing that capabilities developed under PESCO be available to NATO and be "complementary and interoperable."

"Our security is interconnected," the document stipulates, while confirming that "EU efforts will also strengthen NATO." Both will encourage member states that belong to only one of these organisations to participate in the initiatives of the other. Alignment with NATO is expressed in PESCO's founding documents and reiterated by the EU leadership at every opportunity. And on 18th May last, the EU Military Staff was confirmed as a "guest mission partner" of NATO's "combined federated battle laboratories network."

The joint EU-NATO Summit (July 2018) declaration identifies military mobility as a priority, and the EU plans to invest €5.7 billion in the project during the 2021–27 budgetary cycle.

Then there is the nuclear-armed European Intervention Initiative (EII) launched in July 2018. This development is facilitated by the enhanced co-operation provisions of the Lisbon Treaty (Art. 20 TEU). Ten EU states, including France, Germany and Britain, have signed up, prepared to act outside the EU's borders without help from NATO or the US. The initiative involves "joint planning work on crisis scenarios that could 'potentially' threaten EU security." This is a potential vehicle for post Brexit military co-operation outside the EU framework and would combine Europe's only two powers with both the military capacity and the strategic will to use force overseas—Britain and France — with a handful of smaller, but willing, EU states.

But there's also a belt and braces approach implicit in the creation of an 'anchor army' in which currently, the Czech Republic, Romania, Bulgaria, Slovakia and, significantly, the Netherlands have placed significant sections of their armies under German control and command. This army's function is unspecified but is plainly a shadow EU Army in case of the failure of the Commission's plans.

On 13 June 2018, the Commission proposed a new €10.5bn Orwellian "European Peace Facility," an instrument outside the EU's long - term budget, which would improve the EU's ability to "prevent conflicts, build peace, and guarantee international security." Federica Mogherini, said: "We are taking measures that will facilitate the rapid movement of Member States' forces in Europe. Furthermore, with the Commission's support, I am proposing the establishment of a European Peace Facility that will improve the financing of EU military operations and improve our support for actions by our partners."

The fund would facilitate the EU's contributions to "peace operations" led by "partners" such as Somalia and the Central African Republic in the shape of "infrastructure, equipment or military assistance," which Mogherini confirmed could include the purchase of weapons. No wonder Macron, said in April that "Europe has its destiny bound with Africa!"

Only last month, bipartisan legislators in the US passed the National Defence Authorization Act (2018), which includes $6.5 billion to finance the "European Deterrence Initiative," building military capabilities of EU states near Russia, and contributing to the further militarisation of the EU. Other additional funds support an increase in EU/US military cooperation. This, despite member states questioning the commitment of the US to European "security," following Trump's campaign statements.

Overall military spending in EU countries totals some €200 billion annually. Two per cent of GDP has been pledged by the members of PESCO, to be spent on weapons development and procurement.

If Germany alone reaches the agreed target of two per cent of GDP, it will have a military budget much larger than the putative enemy's — Russia's — and that is by 2027. (The 2018 Russian military budget is $55bn, while Germany's is $43bn.) In 2016, the EU 28 spent €206bn, while France spent €43bn and Russia €42bn.

In 2016, Irelands' military spending was the lowest in the EU and one of the lowest in the word at 0.3% of GDP; in real terms around €960m per annum, so, for Irish military expenditure to reach the 2% level demanded, it would have to be increased to unbelievable level of €6bn+ per annum, or half the total national health budget — our biggest budget item! This is absolutely staggering!!

In 2016, the highest levels of military expenditure in the EU were in Estonia (2.4 % of GDP), and Greece (2.1 % of GDP).

Aside from the considerable moral, political and ethical considerations associated with militarisation and the increased risk of conflict, this is an appalling waste of resources at a time when the poor are getting poorer and the rich richer.

The constitutional amendment permitting Lisbon's ratification in Ireland included the sentence: "Ireland affirms its commitment to the European Union…." So, Ireland, a supposedly neutral, independent State has affirmed a constitutional "commitment" to a superior entity made up of other states sharing the common objective of creating an EU army!

Recently, the biennial delegate conference of Connect, Ireland's largest engineering union, unanimously adopted a motion calling for Ireland's immediate withdrawal from PESCO.

This illustrates a growing public awareness that the cost of involvement in PESCO represents a new priority in government expenditure, to the inevitable detriment of public goods such as housing, education and health. This, at a time, when members of the Irish Defence Forces and their families are forced to apply for supplementary income benefits because of poor wages and conditions.

According to the EU's statistics agency, in 2016, 117.5 million people in the EU were threatened with poverty or social exclusion — 23.4 percent of its population; corresponding closely with statistics from 2007. The EU has proven incapable of reducing poverty — particularly in the peripheral states. The concentration of resources in western EU centres of power — and above all in the German hegemonic pole — continue to fuel the EU's ambitions to achieve "global player" status through the creation of an EU military-industrial complex and attendant EU Army in close partnership with NATO. Eventually, all military bases in the EU will effectively be NATO bases.

And last week, Finland brought the number of members of the EII to eleven, while French President Macron, on the centenary of the 'war to end all wars', called for an EU Army — a call supported days later by German Chancellor Merkel in the EU Parliament. Astonishingly, the Commission expressed 'delight'. One shudders to contemplate their sentiments in the event of conflict!

And so, the rush to an EU Army continues at an alarming pace. The much-vaunted EU 'peace project' has morphed into the EU war project, led by former colonial powers eager to plunder the resources of poorer countries. They have issued a call to arms and we must respond with a call to action, while those of us in EU Member States – including Ireland – must ponder and discuss whether we wish to continue to be members of the EU war machine.

Jeannie Toschi Marazzani Visconti
Cominato No Guerra No NATO
Italy

Good morning dear friends,

I am a member of Comitato No Guerra No NATO of Italy. Our Committee is relatively young. We founded it about three years ago. Nevertheless, our petition against US and NATO bases and nuclear bombs was signed by thirty-four thousand followers. We obtained this result by producing and posting on line videos on US bases, nuclear bombs and other contingent issues.

Last night you saw our short film describing US/NATO bases scattered throughout Italian territory. By now you know our situation: Italy hosts 110 US air and naval bases, our ports and airports are at the total disposal of US air and naval forces. Italian military expenses are close to seventy million euros a day. In Aviano and Ghedi air bases, seventy B61 nuclear bombs are sheltered; in 2020 they will be replaced by the B61-12s. These bombs go along with the F35 fighter that we also produce in Cameri, near Novara. From our country, war operations to Yugoslavia, Libya and Syria were launched. The Trident Juncture 2018 war game, taking place in the north of Europe in these days, is controlled by US Admiral James G. Foggo from NATO's South Europe Command in Laco Patria, Naples. Italian territory as a whole is practically a US and NATO base.

All this happens with total silence on the part of the media. People seem absent; they seem not to understand the great danger lingering above our heads. Italy signed the None Nuclear Proliferation Treaty and we want our country to respect it. We want neutrality and peace.

What we propose and we do believe in it, it is a large network involving all associations and movements aiming at the dismantlement of US and NATO bases, because only united we can achieve that result.

Plenary 7:

Africa /AFRICOM

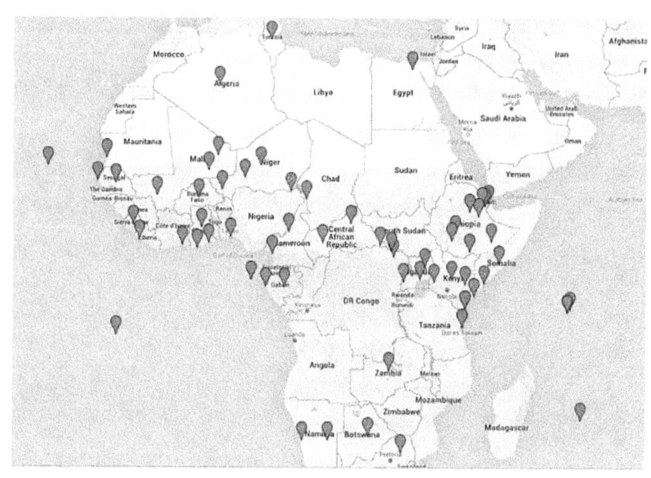

Chair:
Margaret Kimberley
Black Agenda Report
USA

Chair's Opening Remarks

Margaret Kimberley
Editor
Black Agenda Report
USA

My name is Margaret Kimberley and I welcome you all to the AFRI-COM panel of our International Conference Against US and NATO Military Bases. I'm very happy to be here and I'm joined by three great panelists. We will discuss the issue of the military presence of the US on the African continent, which is embodied in AFRICOM. And we'll also talk about the role of other nations in the continuing imperialist scramble for Africa.

AFRICOM, the US Africa command, came into being ten years ago on October 1, 2008 towards the end of the George W. Bush administration. This is its mission statement:

"[AFRICOM] will strengthen our security cooperation with Africa and create new opportunities to bolster the capabilities of our partners in Africa. Africa Command will enhance our efforts to bring peace and security to the people of Africa and promote our common goals of development, health, education, democracy, and economic growth in Africa."

It's all a bit of a joke but that's what they said anyway. It's always placed, interventions and occupations, are always couched in some humanitarian terms, aren't they? That's how they get buy in.

AFRICOM itself came to little attention even though it is an American effort. It flew under the radar pretty much until last year. Last fall, in 2017, four American soldiers were killed in Niger. Most Americans were not aware of AFRICOM, most did not know about Niger. People were afraid to pronounce it, it sounded too much like a slur. But the killing of these soldiers brought AFRICOM into renewed focus. The story unfortunately became a story about Donald Trump and his demeanor and what he said to a widow and what he said to a congresswoman. Americans being who they are the corporate media being what it is focused on those things and the opportunity to talk about AFRICOM was lost.

As Bahman mentioned, in addition to being on the Administrative Committee of United National Antiwar Coalition (UNAC) and an Editor and Senior Columnist of Black Agenda Report, I'm here as one of the Coordinating Committee members of Black Alliance for Peace. Black Alliance for Peace is a young organization founded on April 4, 2017. The date was not a coincidence. That is the date of the assassination of Martin Luther King. It was the 50th anniversary of his speech at Riverside Church in which he publicly denounced the Vietnam war and the 49th anniversary of his assassination.

Black Alliance for Peace "seeks to recapture and redevelop the historic anti-war, anti-imperialist, and pro-peace positions of the radical black movement." Black Alliance for Peace is a very committed member of and a part of this Global Campaign Against US/NATO Military Bases around the world. This year, after the 10th anniversary of AFRICOM's founding, Black Alliance for Peace became the leader of an effort to end AFRICOM and get the US out of Africa. Please take a look at our website at blackallianceforpeace.com and you'll see there a petition that is demanding an end to AFRICOM. We're almost at 1,500 signatures and our goal is to have 10,000 signatures by January 15, which is Dr. King's birthday. As I said, the petition calls for an end to AFRICOM and demands that members in particular of the Congressional Black Caucus take the lead in in doing this, holding hearings and investigating AFRICOM and ending it altogether. All that talk of a blue wave and Democratic control of the House of Representatives is supposed to mean something isn't it?

I'm going to introduce our panel and we're going to have time for questions and answers. Please ask questions, not make statements, and do so within sixty seconds. I plan to call on people who we haven't heard from yet. I'm encouraging those of you who haven't participated yet to do so.

I'm going to introduce our panel and we can get started. In no particular order, I am joined by Anne Atambo. She is the founder and president of the Women's International League for Peace and Freedom, Kenya. She is a women's rights activist and believes that women in Africa are key in reshaping the future of the continent and to insuring sustainable peace and development. She has a background in peace and conflict studies and sociology and a minor in Chinese language from the University of Nairobi. She holds a post graduate certificate in Chinese language and culture from Tianjin University in Tianjin, China, and she speaks Chinese as well.

Chris Matlhako is Coordinator of the South Africa Peace Initiative. The South Africa Peace Initiative is a part of a larger coalition of groups that have a goal of promoting sovereignty and anti-imperialist struggle and progressive international solidarity. Welcome, Chris.

We are also joined by Paul Pumphrey. Paul is a Co-Founder of Friends of the Congo and he has been an organizer and activist for over forty years. In 1998 he co-founded Brothers and Sisters International, a nonprofit organization whose focus is economic development and human rights in the Americas, the Caribbean and Africa. He was a deputy coordinator of the Southern Christian Leadership Council (SCLC) marches on Washington and for Stand for the Children, volunteered with Jesse Jackson's presidential campaigns and Ron Daniels 1992 Presidential campaign. He was a co-founder of the anti-apartheid movement in 1975 and, as I said, Friends of the Congo, which was founded in 2004. He is going to talk to us about the Congo.

Chris Matlhako
Coordinator
South Africa Peace Initiative

It is indeed a great honour to have been invited to take part in this event and to highlight the crucial role of military bases on the African continent — impact and the configuration of societies that have been impacted upon negatively by the consequences of civil wars and military bases.

Both the proliferation and spread of powerful military instruments of the imperialist nations have not only undermined democracy. Emerging post-independent nations' endeavours towards genuine development have been denuded and deformed as a result of influence of the militarism enveloping these countries.

Huge amounts of resources are also spent on military expenditures and shifted away from the demands of social and other key important deliveries required to ensure that ours are societies that encompass the concerns of our societies.

There are US bases, compounds, port facilities and fuel bunkers in thirty-four African countries, including in regional hegemons Kenya, Ethiopia and Algeria. Under the guise of countering terrorism, and through joint partnerships, Washington has infiltrated continental security organisations and has touted the idea of establishing on-the-ground liaison offices. American military officials and policy makers view the continent as a full-scale battlefield in the competition against China, and through promoting regionalism. US officials are successfully circumventing continental institutions, including the African Union (AU). To date, this has not yet been a major factor in interstate conflicts on the continent, but US cooperation has sought to mould partner countries to share its stance on foreign issues. Further, the US uses these bases to carry out activities on other continents; drones operating from Chadelley Base in Djibouti have been deployed in Yemen and Syria, for example. This then inserts African states into conflicts unrelated to them, their regions or the continent.

Disaggregate some of the issues regarding military intervention on the African continent

— fragility of African states

— power of external interests (multinationals)

— the long and inglorious history of intervention runs from colonial and post-colonial struggle through to the Cold War.

There is also the complex, dangerous, unfolding world event, the so-called war on terror:

— the arrival of China and the emergence of regional powers, jostling for influence, has complicated the map.

— disputes around electoral outcomes and subsequent instability and violence invite external intervention.

— the events in and human catastrophe in Cameroun (the Anglophone problem) accompanied by the dead silence of the international community has emboldened dictator Paul Biya, who has ruled Cameroun for two decades.

These bases, especially those maintained by global powers, have impaired the AU from implementing indigenous continental solutions, especially those requiring inclusiveness and mediation. Mali is significant in this regard, especially since the presence of French troops stationed there for Operation Barkhane has stymied efforts by Malian civil society to include the Islamist Ansar Dine (now the Group for the Protection of Islam and Muslims) in the political process, thus prolonging the insurgency in the north. Similarly, the United Arab Emirates (UAE) bases in Somaliland incentivise and formalise the fragmentation of Somalia, with negative regional consequences. In the coming decades, problems such as these will be exacerbated, as countries such as India, Iran and Saudi Arabia construct military bases in African countries, and because the sub-regional coordination mechanisms such as the Multi-National Joint Task Force in the Lake Chad Basin, which have had successes, are more proficient at dealing with cross-border insurgency. It is noteworthy that these initiatives are often continental efforts undertaken by sub-regional states, frequently in opposition to the intentions and programmes of global powers.

There is a great need for Africans to be concerned about these developments and the focus on the creation of bases, because of their impact on the populations of various countries, and the implications for state as well as continental sovereignty. Diego Garcia, the base that set the trend for this phenomenon in Africa, illustrates the rather drastic potential impacts of these developments. The island's population has been reduced to one lacking rights and freedoms, with many of its members forcibly removed from their homes and deported — most to Mauritius and the Seychelles, not allowed the right to return. Further, the presence of the base has ensured that the AU has little influence over the island; it is still *de facto* ruled as a British territory.

Similarly, the 'global war on terror', coupled with the rise of China, has seen global powers seeking to re-enter or strengthen their presence on the continent, with negative consequences. Both the US and France have constructed new bases in Africa, with China, the UAE and Saudi Arabia following suit. Under the guise of fighting terrorism, they often have other interests, such as France's bases in Niger, which are more about an attempt to protect French interests around Niger's vast uranium resources.

Hotspots:

Twin hotspots are the Sahel and the Horn of Africa — "It's where Europe touches Africa, and where Africa touches the Middle East."

Sahel:
The Sahel controls the migration route that conveys young men and women across the Mediterranean.

The war in Libya has contributed to soft borders and pathways for light arms, which reached fundamentalists like Boko Haram and al-Shabab and others on the continent more easily.

It is a 'zone of instability' where al-Qaeda, so-called Islamic State and Boko Haram operate.

From across the region, US drones and French soldiers have joined African armies to push the militants into remote hinterlands.

These alliances have also given leaders like Idriss Deby in Chad and Ismail Guelleh in Djibouti some regime security and a pass on their dodgy human rights record.

Horn of Africa:

Djibouti lies on the Bab-el-Mandeb Strait, a gateway to the Suez Canal — one of the world's busiest shipping lanes.

It is also a waypoint between Africa, India and the Middle East and makes a lot of money from hosting seven (7) armies — America, China, Italy, France, Germany, Japan, Spain and soon Saudi Arabia.

The lease on the only permanent US military base in Africa, Camp Lemonnier, Djibouti, is $63 million a year.

China (it is building its first overseas military base) is constructing its own facility at the other end of the Gulf of Tadjoura, Djibouti, and gets a bargain at $20 million.

China, it must be borne mind, has a $12 billion investment in Djibouti, including a new port, airports and the Ethiopian-Djibouti rail line.

The base will have the capacity to house several thousand troops and is expected to help provide security for China's interests in the rest of the Horn of Africa.

Only Iran seems to have been refused a berth in Djibouti.

Light and Small Arms and Crises of Instability
The Inter-Imperialist Rivalries

South Africa's sale of small and light arms to the Saudi Arabian regime could also be contributing towards the escalation of death and destruction in Yemen.

The UN Security Council on Thursday voted unanimously to extend the United Nations Multidimensional Integrated Stabilization Mission in the Central African Republic (MINUSCA) for a month. The mandate for the mission was due to expire at midnight on Thursday. Speaking before the Council, Russia warned France that it must put aside "parochial national interests" and recognize Russia's peace efforts in the Central African Republic (CAR).

— France and Russia are now bickering over the right to oversee this mandate in the CAR.
— Russia had also convened a meeting of warring factions in Khartoum to work out a framework for peace in the CAR.

However, there have been positive developments in the Horn of Africa:

— securing peace between Eritrea and Ethiopia
— lifting of sanctions against Eritrea

— the return to normality in Zimbabwe in the post-Mugabe period is cautiously welcomed.

However, the outstanding elections in the Democratic Republic of the Congo (DRC) have increased the imperialist interventionist agenda and could explode into another devastating war with serious consequences for vulnerable women and children.

NB: One of the key outcomes we must consider coming out of this Conference to try to develop links between where the bases are and the areas where there are consequences — those who feel the consequences of war.

Ann Atambo
President
Women's International League for Peace and Freedom – Kenya

I grew up in Nairobi, Kenya. We are famous for a few things, like running, for example. It is important to note, however, that this special gene evaded me, and as a result, I cannot run to save my dear life.

But one of the things for which we are lesser known is something that could perhaps be significant to the participants of this conference. In 2013, Kenyans who were tortured by the colonial forces in the years leading up to Kenya's independence received reparations worth around twenty million pounds sterling. While this, to no extent whatsoever, qualifies the trauma, loss of lives and destruction that ensued, and whose ripple effects we suffer still as a nation, some headlines still went ahead and termed them as "PAYOUTS." Payouts?! And to them I say, dignity does not have a price tag. And so, we stick to reparations.

While this state of emergency denied us precious moments with our fathers, grandfathers and forefathers, sixty years on, a tall and proud statue stands in the center of Kenya, the capital city, as a sign of honour for the fighters that bravely paved the way for this Kenyan to be up here on this stage at this moment, in this hall. It signifies victory from physical chains.

And with that, I express my gratitude for the conveners of this hallmark event, to the Peace and Neutrality Alliance, to the Coalition Against U.S. Foreign Military Bases, to all the honorable ladies and gentlemen in this room. I salute you. And to every soul that has long carried high the banner of the noble course with which we convene here today. I salute you.

The countries in East Africa have quite a relationship with NATO.

From the unfortunate and ruthless colonial histories to the newly redefined relationships by way of bases sprawled all over the continent. The men in that picture that you saw, in quaint little hats all around the distressed Mau Mau fighter were the KAR. Aptly called, the Kings African Riffles. The history of the KAR dates back to 1890. They were formed by the Imperial British East African Company, and together with other agents, namely the Uganda Rifles, the East African Rifles and the Central African Rifles formed a regiment that acted as defenders of the British empire.

The regiment fought and I quote this from the Kings African Rifle Association, "in both World Wars against the armies of Germany, Italy, Vichy France and Japan, gaining proud battle honours: British Somaliland, Abyssinia, Madagascar and Burma. It then played a leading role in post war operations against the Communists in Malaya and the Mau Mau in Kenya, before the final chapter in the early sixties, when, as each nation achieved independence, the regiment divided, to … PLEASE NOTE … re-emerge at the heart of their national armies, where our customs and traditions still flourish"

From the founding of these regiments, years on, to what are now NATO foreign military bases, since 2005, NATO has sent more than 40,000 civilian and military personnel to the continent, while the EU has sent more than 10,000.

But, what makes a nation gullible to such provisions?

1. Political Structures: For the continuous furthering of these atrocious endeavors, deals and the power of the pen, both steadily rely on a hand that is willingly swayed. The powers that be and the interests they uphold are reflected by the policies pursued.

2. Historical Ties: The colonial ties stretch on and will haunt the generations to come. With innovative re-imaginations of the same old outfits of oppression. This is espoused by issues as simple as the language spoken as the official medium of communication by countries in Africa (enter Anglophone and Francophone countries) . These historical ties then morph into continually strengthened militarized relationships.

3. Economic dependency: The political consequences of economic dependency costs recipient states whatever sort of autonomy over their national development they could have had. In such cases, foreign aid acts as a foreign policy tool, furthering the interests of the donor nation at the expense of the beneficiaries.

Last but not least,

4. Geographical significance: Countries that stand in the regions and show promise of bearing significant strategic benefits, have their lands used as playgrounds for the warships.

Going back to the regiments that we spoke of earlier, four provisions can all be summed up by the words of the official historian of the KAR Lieutenant Colonel, Dr. H Moyse, and I quote "No regiment has ever been more intimately connected with the territories in which it marched and fought, or with the people from whom it recruited."

These for me stand as the core fundamental provisions that make up the recipe for a subservient nation-state. But Africa has its own set challenges that pull us further down into this militarization abyss. In the book *The Bottom Billion,* by Paul Collier, he points out five things that make African nations vulnerable.

1. The natural resources trap. Natural resources attract the most lewd of corporations onto the continent that dispense with morality in the face of capitalism and its ugly head. Resource extraction is a multi-billion dollar industry and having a subservient continent is good for business.

2. Being landlocked: Poor countries that are landlocked find themselves at the mercy of more geographically strategic nations that have access to ports, especially on a continent that has a struggling transport system between nations in the region.

3. Conflict Trap: Civil wars and military coups have long plagued the continent. Countries with a low level of income and slow economic growth are most prone to civil war. Once the cycle of civil war and violence begins in a country, it is often difficult to break free of it, because it makes a country more susceptible to falling into yet another civil war.

4. Bad governance: Bad leadership and corruption plagues a nation because of the rhetoric that is created and the fear that is brewed amongst the people. For many years I would have to explain, apologetically, that when we spoke of dictators in African countries, we the people did not necessarily vote for them. But since the election of a certain world leader in what was once heralded as the lighthouse of the free world, I can safely say that we all now understand how some people, unqualified and unpopular as they may be, still end up as President.

So what happens in a continent that is rendered vulnerable by its own leaders and external powers. In Swahili we say "*Fahali wawili wakipigana, ni nyasi inaumia,*" which basically translates as: when two bulls fight, the grass pays for it, what with all the huffing and puffing and stamping on the grass.

That signifies that we weakest of the weak, suffer the most.

Women in Africa have long survived in a patriarchal system. And in a similar light, increased militarisation and the presence of these military bases in Africa only reinforces their plight.

Indeed, there is a growing proliferation of military bases on the continent. For example, Djibouti hosts many military bases, with France, Italy, Japan and even China having military bases there. Turkey has a military base in Eritrea, while India has facilities in Mauritius and the Seychelles.

But what does it really mean to have military bases in one's country? What does it mean to live next to a military base on the continent of Africa? In Kenya, the US military has a base in Isiolo. Isiolo is in the northern part of Kenya, bordering Somalia. Somalia has had an interesting history with the US. Since the Battle of Mogadishu in 1993 that involved US troops with the support of the United Nations Mission in Somalia (UNOSOM), where lives were lost and civil unrest has reigned supreme in the country.

The result of this civil unrest and altercation was the development of Dadaab refugee camp, which is hosted in Kenya. Kenya has been playing host to this camp, which is the second largest complex of its kind in the world.

As a country, Kenya has paid the price for being a partisan of the US mission in Somalia. On 7th August 1998, my father came home with a bloodied shirt. The US Embassies in Nairobi and Tanzania had been bombed simultaneously. Two hundred twenty four people lost their lives in Nairobi, while eleven people died in Tanzania.

My father did not work for the US Embassy. He worked in an adjacent building close to the one that was targeted. My mother, who was heavily expectant with our youngest sibling, said she would have been on that street, but something delayed her and she ended up taking a detour, and possibly saving hers and my unborn brother's life.

Traumatic as it was, my father was a very lucky man. I have an aunt that worked in the same company as my father. Hers is a different case. A lady that was steadily rising in the corporate field, her promising career was cut short. Not physically, but mentally. She hasn't been able to get back to work and I remember seeing her trotting about, a changed woman. Her young family was obviously changed as well by the impact of that bombing.

On Saturday 21st September, 2013, seventy-one people where killed in a shopping mall. The non-fatal injuries were as high as 175. On April 2nd 2015, gunmen stormed a university in Garissa, killing 147 students and injuring seventy-six more. This was in retaliation for having Kenyan bases on Somali land. Please note, that we get additional support from the US to facilitate these joint missions into Somali and other African nations.

And so having foreign military bases, and being allies to these forces, comes at a dear cost. Yet no one is held accountable. We, the civilians, are subjected to undue trauma and terror, for fighting battles that are not even ours to start with.

Additionally, these uniformed gears, wielding big machines, inadvertently cause a cultural desensitization of what authority looks like. And so, it only leads to more militarization and the infiltration of small arms and light weapons resulting from surplus armoury.

This year in Kenya, government expenditure on defence and intelligence hit the one billion dollar mark. It is set to rise next year. This poses a risk to the citizens of the nation-state. Thus two recommendations that should be highlighted are, first, an end to end psycho-social support systems and, secondly, the engagement of the public in the decision making process, both of which are seldom the practice in Africa. And so, if the aforementioned suggestions do not produce a moral result, please remember, that just like the Mau Mau events, history will judge us harshly.

I will end with two quotes from my favourite pan-Africanist, Kwameh Nkrumah:

(i) The independence of Ghana is meaningless unless it is linked with the liberation of the African continent.

(ii) Countrymen, the task ahead is great indeed and heavy is the responsibility.

And yet, it is a noble and glorious challenge — a challenge which calls for
the courage to dream,
the courage to believe,
the courage to dare,
the courage to do,
the courage to envision,
the courage to fight,
the courage to work,
the courage to achieve — to achieve the highest of excellencies and the fullest greatness of man.

Dare we ask for more in life.

And so I didn't greet you in my name. I stand as one, but we are a multitude. I represent the voice of the women who lost their husbands in the war against terror, the children maimed by deserted artillery scattered by foreign military personnel on the continent.

And we stand here to say, enough with the foreign military bases on our lands.

Paul Pumphrey
Friends of the Congo
USA

Good morning. My name is Paul Pumphrey and I am with an organisation by the name of Friends of the Congo. When we look at Africom and Africa, as well as the European military involvement in Africa, we must also see it as a geo-strategic move for looting the resources of Africa, and today more so than ever because the major resources for our electronics industry and for our hi-tech industry, those resources are found in huge quantities in Africa and no place in Africa more than the Congo. So basically we are looking at a situation wherein the United States historically has played a behind-the-scenes role in Africa and now finds itself in a position where it has to play a more overt role militarily in Africa.

Often people think that the United States' involvement in the Congo is something of a recent phenomena, but the reality is that United States has been involved with the Congo for over 125 years. Let us remember that King Leopold of the Belgians never went to Africa. Nor did anybody from Belgium survey the Congo. So explain to me how all of a sudden King Leopold could request control over the greater Congo at the 1884/85 Conference in Berlin when Europe was dividing up Africa and when they didn't know where the Congo was?

It was clear to me that the United States played that role. The United States needed rubber, and they knew that if Great Britain or France, the more industrialized parts of Europe, got control over the rubber plantations or the wild rubber trees inside the Congo, the US would have to pay a higher price for the rubber. So the United States cut a deal with King

Leopold, a fairly undeveloped European head of state, to claim control at that conference for the Congo region. And so the United States was able to get the cake and eat it too because no matter what kind of crimes that were committed inside the Congo to force the Congolese to harvest more rubber, the blame went to King Leopold, not to the United States.

A similar situation happened in apartheid South Africa. They used the Boers as a means to get the blame for the atrocities of apartheid, but interesting enough where did the concept of Bantustans come from? I would definitely believe it came from Indian reservations in the United States. And so the United States has historically played a role in Africa from behind the scenes.

But because of a new element in the geopolitical and economic arena of Africa known as China, the United States now has to play a more overt role. The United States had been involved in the Congo for over 125 years and in that period of time never built one school, never built one hospital, never even built a road. But it did supply Mobutu with hundreds of, actually hundreds of millions, and even billions, of dollars worth of military equipment to keep him in power inside the Congo so that they would loot the riches of the Congo.

But then that changed when they discovered the powers of coltan, coltan being a mineral that is used in every type of sophisticated electronic equipment on earth today. And they figured out that the Congo had 64% of all the coltan in the world. So whoever controls coltan in the Congo controls not only the electronic industry but the financial might of the world. At that point they realised that the puppet they had put in power in the Congo was too greedy and that if he had figured out the value of coltan there was no way US corporations would get this raw material cheaply. So they sent envoys to Mobutu and said, hey guy, you have got to leave. We have given you thirty-two years of power where you were allowed to loot the country and do our dirty work but now you have to go. Mobutu said no, this is my country and under the constitution of this country I am the owner of this country, how dare you tell me leave my own home. So they had to move to Plan B, which was to militarily take him out.

Interestingly enough, the United States had only one ally that they could use to carry out that mission, who happened to be Museveni in Uganda and so they decided to get him some support. After all Uganda is, what, one twentieth the size of the Congo, maybe one tenth the size of the population of the Congo. It would not look possible that this one little small country could take on the Congo so the United States orchestrated a war in Rwanda. How did they do that? They recruited the head of intelligence of the Ugandan army who happened to be a young man by the name of Paul Kagame and flew him to Fort Leavenworth, Kansas, and trained him and recruited him to work on behalf of the CIA. Now the interesting thing about Paul Kagame was that at the age of three his family was pushed out of Rwanda and ended up in Uganda. So of course his first language was English, not French. When he went back to Uganda he recruited other Rwandans, who had helped Musevini win his military coup in Uganda a number of years earlier. They began to go across the border from Uganda into Rwanda and attack police stations, military barracks, schools, et cetera.

Then George Bush the first lost the 1992 Presidential election to a guy by the name of Bill Clinton. So when Clinton comes to power what does he do? He calls for a peace negotiation between the warring factions in Rwanda and Burundi and he invites the President of the Congo, Mobutu, the President of Kenya, the President of Rwanda and the president of Burundi to come to Tanzania so that they can have a pow-wow to see if they could meet with these rebels and resolve the problem. They did that and they came up with an agreement. The US provided an aircraft for the President of Rwanda and Burundi to fly back home and, interestingly enough, a US air missile blew them out of the air. That is what led to what most people now know as the Rwandan genocide. Convenient huh?

Then we look a little further at how the United States uses its military might. They now have two countries that can push Mobutu out of power. By the way, Mobutu and the President of Kenya refused to go to that meeting so Mobutu is still alive at this point. Rwanda lost 800,000 people in its civil war. Let me make something very clear here: out of the 800,000 that lost their lives in Rwanda, every independent study of that war shows that at least 600,000 of them were Hutus, not Tutsis, so it wasn't a genocide against Tutsis.

Secondly, you had a situation where the newly formed government of Rwanda in 1994 lines up with the government of Uganda in 1996, about a year and a half later. The Rwandan army were mostly people who were members of the Ugandan army, who were Tutsis and had come back into the new government set up after the civil war in Rwanda. So they had come into Rwanda for the first time or after maybe, like Paul Kagame, and left at the age of three to five to ten years old. They had been out of the country for many years. Now they were going to be able to create an army matched up with the army of Uganda and to march across the border from the eastern part of the Congo to Kinshasa to overthrow Mobutu. Now understand the Congo at this point: the Congo has no roads between the eastern part of the country and Kinshasa. Uganda has no air force and Rwanda has no air force. So how in the world did these armies make it to Kinshasa?

I have to share a personal point here. I was cofounder of the Anti-Apartheid Movement USA and in that role I did a number of speaking engagements around the United States with a gentlemen from Namibia by the name of Theo-Ben Gurirab, who, when Namibia got its independence, became their first foreign minister. In 2006, I paid a visit to Ben in Namibia. I told him I had just come from the Congo and he said funny you should tell me you came from the Congo. Let me tell you what happened in 1998. In 1998, the person that was installed as President after they got rid of Mobutu, in 1996, was a guy by the name of Laurent-Désiré Kabila, who had been a Congolese freedom fighter who had fought against Mobutu some thirty years earlier, but had been out of the country for at least twenty-eight years and didn't really understand what was going on in the country when he was installed as President, supposedly by Congolese rebels but in reality by the Ugandan and Rwandan armies. After he returned to his country, he began to realise that the governments of Uganda and Rwanda were stealing more minerals and selling it on the international market from the Congo than he was able to sell on the international market. And being a nationalist, he decided, uh-uh, that is not going to happen. He said to the armies and governments of Uganda and Rwanda, thank you very much but goodbye, you are going to have to go home. He created his own army of Congolese that escorted Uganda and Rwanda troops to their borders and told them to stay on their side of the border.

So now he has a Congolese army along the border in 1998 and of course the United States decided this was not acceptable because they didn't know what this guy might do. He might just be selling to the highest bidder, which might mean China. The US wanted control over those minerals. So the second war started in 1998 inside the Congo. Interestingly enough, the armies of Uganda and Rwanda ended up in the central part of the Congo yet the Congolese army is along the border between Uganda and Rwanda, and they didn't march across the border and they don't have an air force. Ben explained to me how they got there. He said that the Congolese army could not prevent them from reaching Kinshasa so the President of the Congo called Zimbabwe, called Namibia and called Angola and asked for military assistance, and they provided it. They defeated the Ugandan/Rwandan troops in the central part of the Congo. Ben, the foreign minister of Namibia, and the foreign minister of Zimbabwe were flying in a helicopter surveying this situation because they knew they were responsible for the defeated troops when all of a sudden they got a telephone call from the deputy foreign minister of Zimbabwe saying Madeleine Albright wants to talk to you, boss. He says tell her I am busy. The deputy foreign minister says no, she is calling every five minutes. She wants to talk to you now. So he takes the call and puts her on the speaker phone. Ben is listening to the conversation. Madeleine Albright is asking for permission for the United States to be given air rights so they can send transport planes back into the Congo to pick up the troops from Uganda and Rwanda, the ones they had left off.

So if anyone has a question as to what was going on in the war in the Congo where Rwanda/Uganda killed, according to a UN estimate, from 1996 to 2006, over six million people, of which over three million were children below the age of five, we can understand what happened.

So here is the US government coming to a conclusion that they could no longer depend on Uganda and Rwanda and other troops to do their thing. So George Bush decides to start the African Command so the United States could, for the first time, overtly take the lead role in controlling what is going on in Africa. However, George Bush wasn't a very popular person amongst African leaders so he was allowed to have only three military bases built in Africa during his administration. So what does big business do in the United States? They put their money behind a guy by the name of Barack Obama. And for the eight years that Obama was in office, the African Command went from three military bases to eighty-four military bases. And many of my friends wondered why I was opposed to Obama becoming President of the United States, but that is the reality.

So we have a situation now where a map was shown earlier of US military bases all over the place and I have to say to people: understand something. What comes first, terrorism or US involvement? Look at Afghanistan. In 1978, the King was overthrown and the US and Saudi Arabia first started supporting the warlords of Afghanistan. But then they realised the warlords were only interested in taking back control over the land that they lost when the King was overthrown and they stopped fighting. The US and Saudi Arabia figured they needed soldiers, people who could fight over the long haul. And so they started recruiting people from all over the world, you know, to carry out a war against the great Satan of the Soviet Union in

Afghanistan. So what did they do? They worked with Pakistan and the CIA, and Saudi Arabia provided over forty billion dollars in cash. That is how Osama Bin Laden from Saudi Arabia ends up over in a cave, if you want to believe he was in a cave, in Afghanistan. A man who had kidney disease and had to undergo dialysis. You could see that, right, him on a kidney machine in a cave somewhere? But that is the story they tell us. That is what led to the building of Al Qaeda and later on to the building of the different groups in Africa as well as in the Middle East.

It is clear that this is a real problem and it is a problem led by the capitalist desires of the United States. And, of course, Europe are good lapdogs. We used to call Tony Blair Bush's poodle, but that is the reality. So you have this grab for the wealth of the minerals.

They tell you places like the Congo are poor. Let me address that issue. The Congo has an estimated $24 trillion worth of minerals. It has the second largest rain forest in the world — the second largest rain forest in the world — but not only that, it has the ability because of the Congolese River and that rainfall that, if captured with hydroelectric dams, could produce enough electricity to meet all the electricity needs of the continent of Africa from Cairo to Capetown. In addition, because of its rainfall and its fertile land, it could produce enough food to feed over nine billion people, this one country, more than the world's population, which is currently seven billion. Yet they tell us it is a poor country and that we need to raise money to help those poor people. No, we need to stop the looting.

Thank you.

Plenary 8:

CLOSING SESSION

Chairs:

Bahman Azad
Coalition Against US Foreign Military Bases
USA

Roger Cole
Peace and Neutrality Alliance
Ireland

Chair's Opening Remarks

Bahman Azad
Coalition Against US Foreign Military Bases
USA

We are forming groups on the basis of the regional plenaries that we had. We are asking the participants from the same region to get together to discuss and share with each other information about their anti-bases activities, and if possible, develop a plan for coordinating their regional activities.

We ask each group to select someone from their group to report back to the closing plenary.

One thing I should mention: We are not asking for specific proposals for action from our regional meetings. I am sure there will be hundreds of them and all will be good proposals. However, at this conference we cannot come up with concrete proposals for every region. What we are asking you to do is to give a report to the plenary about the important issues of your region so that everybody learns about the main problems caused by the US/ NATO bases in your region.

We will be back here at 2:30 sharp to hear your reports.

Thank you very much.

Special Remarks Regarding Julian Assange
Mairead Maguire

I am very reluctant to take up what is very precious time to you but I have a favour to ask of you on behalf of a very, very good friend of mine about whom I'm deeply concerned. My friend's name is Julian Assange and Julian Assange is within the Ecuadorian Embassy in London. Many of you already know Julian. I'm afraid unless we make Julian Assange's picture and his story a household name Julian Assange will die in an American prison. He will be arrested and imprisoned for a long time, up to forty five years, maybe longer, and will even face the death penalty. I know we would all like to live as peace activists in a magical world where we all have peace. Of course that is our dream but we have to face reality. We are facing people and governments who are ruthless and who will silence the truth. We need in our world today, more than anything, people who will tell the truth and unfortunately many of them pay a very high price for telling that truth but we witness that in prisons all over the world. Truth tellers who will die in their prisons and their names never known but they stood by their consciences and for the sake of humanity they told the truth to help humanity.

Julian Assange is such a truth teller. Eight years ago through WikiLeaks, as a producer together with the WikiLeaks team, he carried stories of the horrors of what was happening in Afghanistan when from the skies American soldiers and others, their allies, were killing innocent people on the ground. He told the truth. He told the truth about corporations in America and other countries that are abusing people's lives and destroying their lands. For telling that truth he has been charged by the American Government with espionage. Espionage in America carries the death penalty.

When Ecuador gave Julian Assange sanctuary six years ago, they were very good to him because they protected him. They gave him Ecuadorian citizenship to protect him because he doesn't even have at the moment his Australian passport. To the shame of the Australian Government they have ignored the life of Julian Assange inside the Ecuadorian Embassy. They won't even renew, to date, his passport. The Australian Government has a moral responsibility as have all our governments, to stand up for their citizen, to renew his passport and to see that he is safely, if he wishes, taken back to his home in Australia.

And what is happening to Julian inside the Ecuadorian Embassy? I visited him twice. Can you imagine? A small room where you can hardly move and where currently he is not allowed e-mails, the website, not allowed out in the sun. Six years as a prisoner. He has never seen daylight or had exercise. Is there another prisoner in the world being treated like Julian Assange, a man of truth? Is there? Can you think of one? No. Prisoners, and I've been in many prisons, they give them their right to outside air and exercise. Julian has no such right.

His mother made a beautiful appeal last week, appealing for her son's life and for us to do something. Please listen to Christine Assange's appeal from a mother. She says:

"My son's life is in danger. He is slowly being destroyed mentally and physically. His life is in danger. Do something. Please do something."

When the American Government sent one of their ambassadors to the Ecuadorian Embassy a couple of months ago a deal was done between America and Ecuador and the deal is that Assange will be handed over to the UK Government if he steps outside the embassy. They will hand him over to America, which will take him to a grand jury trial there and he will disappear like so many of our other wonderful activists. Mordechai Vanunu — there are people as old as me who remember Vanunu — held inside Israel to this day because Israeli Governments, after 28 years, can hold Vanunu. Why? Because we forget and we forget their names and their sacrifices and they become names in history.

Please let us not, as his friends say we will, forget Julian Assange. We will raise his profile, his name and his story so that the American Government, the Ecuadorian Government, who sold him out, the British Government, who have long since sold him out, will know it is to the shame of the people in those countries and those worlds. We will remember Julian Assange and Mordechai Vanunu, our heroes of truth.

Report from Regional Meeting on North America

David Swanson reporting from the North American group where we had about twenty-eight people from the United States and Canada and essentially the same discussion you just heard reported, which may have happened in a half dozen places around this room, and we will each report it back to each other.

But we talked mostly about April 4th, 2019, about NATO's plan to celebrate itself in Washington DC and about the fact that that is a date that should belong to the history of Dr Martin Luther King and his work of non-violent activist opposition to militarism. As you all know, and four or five more people will tell you, that is the date in 1968 when Dr. King was assassinated and the date exactly one year earlier when he gave his most famous and eloquent speech against militarism and against the "triplets" as he described it, of militarism, racism and extreme materialism, which makes it a date that we think will facilitate the outreach to forming that broad coalition the need for which we have just heard about. So we are working on that.

We also talked about the need to work on education in the United States, around the world, of US Congressmen, new US Congress members, etc., etc., between now and April 4th about what NATO is and what it does, education that debunks the myths that support NATO. We talked about April being a month when groups around the world, including in the United States, oppose the use of taxes for the commission of mass murder and the need for education around the financial trade offs and so forth. We talked about doing online webinars and offline events, possibly days of education events everywhere on certain days between now and April 4th, webinars that people in this room and elsewhere from around the world could be part of by leading and participating in.

There are a number of committees already setup working on April 4th in Washington DC and the days leading up to it, March 30th, the Saturday, the weekend events, up to the Thursday of April 4th, and we talked about forming some additional committees to work on education plans and communication plans and so forth. The myths of NATO that need debunking include "Russia gate" as it is called in the United States, all the lies about Russia and the need to inform people that the preferable alternative to NATO is not a Euro military. We talked about making an interactive map with all the NATO countries and all the NATO bases and all the NATO wars, and honest information about them at the click of a switch.

We want to reach out to everyone else in this room, who was not in our group discussion, to encourage you to get in touch with us to be part of coming to Washington in April, of doing solidarity events in cities around the world at the same time related to shutting down NATO. We have a number of groups and websites I can direct you to. I handed around a flier but there is a website "notonato.org," that World Beyond War and others have setup. The United National Antiwar Coalition (UNAC) and a number of other groups have setup a website, no2NATO2019.org.

You can also look at the Black Alliance for Peace. They are working on this as well. We are trying to get everybody to work together to the fullest extent possible, but there is going to be a rally at the White House, probably on Saturday, 30th March. There are going to be events every day leading up to 4th April. We are going to have conferences, rallies, non-violence training, art creation, giant puppet and art creation projects and non-violent resistance and civil disobedient actions and actions at embassies, and actions at the State Department. So there is a lot to be planned. Please get in touch with us if you want to be involved or if we can help with what you are doing elsewhere.

Very briefly, we also talked about UNAC and other groups, including a group from Sweden working to advance the cause of solidarity events everywhere on May 2nd, so soon after April 4th - May 2nd being the anniversary of the massacre in Odessa in 2014 in which the United States, and the coup in the Ukraine, had a part. The 2nd May event is intended to push back against the Neo-Nazis in the Ukraine that the United States' Government actually trains, supports and arms, and who, in turn, train American Neo-Nazis, who come to my town of Charlottesville, Virginia, and demonstrate for fascism with Ukrainian training.

So at the Ukrainian Embassy in Washington DC on May 2nd and anywhere else that events, small or large, can be created. There are many other projects being worked on in the United States, including local city resolutions on military spending, the sanctions on Venezuela, the trips to everywhere and a week of actions against the militarization of the border about a week from now.

And we shared contact information amongst ourselves and would like to share contact information with everyone here, if that can be arranged. I would like there to be a structure for people who want to help anywhere in the world and for activists in the US or in Washington DC, in particular, to get in touch with each other.

Thank you.

Report from Regional Meeting on the Middle East

Hello, my name is Reem Farha. Following last night's discussion on the Middle East, the first issue we raised was the question of Palestine. The two of us were not unanimous about the two opinions that were discussed. This is my opinion: I am in favour of a two state solution without intervention from outside two states and full solidarity with the Palestinian people. The second issue we discussed was the withdrawal of all foreign military bases from the Middle East, including the naval fleets from all over the Mediterranean Sea, the Persian Gulf and so on.

In regard to Syria we agreed that all violence must be stopped immediately. We also agreed on the withdrawal of all foreign military forces from Syria, including the mercenaries, to pave the way for a political solution for Syria and democratic elections under UN auspices or control; UN control would be best.

In regard to the entire Middle East, we would like all of the states there to establish friendly relations and not to intervene in each other's affairs. We agreed on an immediate end to the war on Yemen and that immediate humanitarian help should be provided to the people in Yemen followed by a political solution. This also applies to Libya where the war must be stopped and a political solution agreed. In our opinion, if the wars in the Middle East are not stopped, there is no chance of a democratic solution or democratic processes within the Middle Eastern countries.

Thank you.

Report from Regional Meeting on Africa

Our breakout group discussed Africa with people from all over the world, from Chad, the Congo, Germany, Ireland, Kenya, South Africa, the US and the UK. We talked about many things but we focussed on preventing the expansion of the US, NATO and other countries into Africa.

We talked about information gathering. I will disseminate all the communication information, e mail information, so that we can be in touch with one another. We talked about identifying groups on the continent who are allies, about amplifying their voices and making sure that none of us from outside the continent of Africa try to impose anything on people who are living with the situations that we discussed.

We talked about making Africa a zone of peace while acknowledging that African nations have contradictions of their own, challenges of their own, and about making connections, acknowledging that there are often collaborations between the "leadership" of African countries and powerful nations outside that create the problems that we discussed at this conference.

We talked about what we can each do in our own countries, about what those who are from the US and Europe can do to try to stop the interference in Africa, the interventions, the invasions, and the occupations by their governments and to use their voices. We talk a lot about being from democracies, which isn't always true anyway, but as far as it is true, we aim to do what we can to influence people and the leadership in our countries.

We talked about supporting political parties and groups in Africa. One of the examples we discussed is the role of the German Peace Movement. Africom is headquartered in Germany. The German Peace Movement could co-ordinate opposition to Africom.

We talked about the petition on the Back Alliance for Peace website. We also discussed the need for signatures in relation to Africom on the change.org web site (search for Africom) for which I thank you in advance.

We discussed how Black Alliance for Peace is developing research teams to talk about some of the issues that we explored, one of which was the issue of gender and militarization and how it impacts societies.

We talked about exploitation, the looting, the theft of resources — those issues came up again and again — and we hope to find ways to speak to those issues in the future.

Thank you.

Report from Regional Meeting on Central and South America

The Latin American and Caribbean group was made up of delegates from Argentina, Brazil, Colombia, Cuba, Puerto Rico, and also friends from Canada, the Czech Republic and the US. We discussed ideas to strengthen communication in the region and talked about the activities that each country or each organisation is organising. Also, projects for education for a culture of peace in the region were brought up by the Argentinian and Columbian comrades and we prioritised some issues that are really of concern to us now in the region. They include the rising threats against Venezuela and the need to support the Venezuelan people in defending their Bolivarian revolution and their sovereignty, of course.

We also discussed the Colombia situation with the Peace Agreement falling apart, the para militarism continuing to kill social leaders and members of the Revolutionary Armed Forces of Colombia — People's Army (FARC) and others who are involved in the uprising there. Also of course, Colombia's relations with the US and NATO and the blockade against Cuba were on our list of priorities. One of the top priorities was the return of the Guantánamo Bay to the Cuban people with the removal of the US naval base there.

We also would like to emphasise the 60th anniversary of the Cuban Revolution, which was also one of our priorities. Puerto Rico, which is still a colony of the United States, was one of our concerns as well. We also wish to highlight the fact that Argentina and Brazil have reactionary and very subservient governments that are aligned to the US, with new military bases in Argentina, including a base in one of the biggest water resources in the world, the Guarani Aquifer, which is shared between Argentinia, Paraguay, and Brazil.

In Brazil, the Neo-Nazi element elected to the Presidency was highlighted as was the willingness of the President to negotiate with the United States about the space base in Alcântara and to surrender Brazil's sovereignty over the base.

And the seminar in Guantánamo, the 60th Seminar For Peace and the Abolition of all Military Bases, was discussed. The President of the Cuban Movement for the Peace and Solidarity of the Peoples (MOVPAZ) informed us about the programme. He is here to tell you about the programme of the seminar and he is again inviting you to look at it and to participate if you can.

Those are the main points. Thank you. Again, just to say that we appreciate the effort and the chance to be here, discussing all these priorities with you.

Thank you again.

Report from Regional Meeting on Asia/Pacific

Our Group was in reality a Pacific group. We had representatives from Okinawa, from the Philippines, from Australia and from the US.

We agreed that we would setup a Pacific Peace Network. So, as of today, we will have a Pacific Peace Network and we will meet regularly online.

We will share information about what is going on in each of our countries and we will aim to also promote events that are happening in the region.

For example, the International League of People Struggles is having a conference in June 2019 in Hong Kong and the organisation that I represent, IPAN in Australia, is having a conference in Darwin where we will be having speakers from the Philippines, possibly from Okinawa again, as we have had at previous conferences.

We would love to have a representative from Indonesia and to build up the solidarity of people's movements in the region in which we live and that is so pivotal to continued American control and military intervention. So I will just keep it brief, I would like also to say thank you very much to the organisers.

It has been an amazing effort on your part. I know that you have told me that it took seven months of full time work, and I don't think you will be doing it again next time. But it has been wonderful to be with so many like minded people and to share that solidarity with each other.

Thank you.

Report from Regional Meeting on Europe

There was a general consensus that the conference had been a success and the meeting thanked the organisers for the initiative and work in bringing the conference to fruition.

The need for a European Network of Peace Groups linked *via* email, Google Groups, or other secure social media system was stressed.

The meeting proposed that there be a dedicated European section on the No US/NATO Foreign Military Bases website if this is technically and organisationally possible.

Within Europe there are three distinct, but linked, situations that we need to confront:

1. There are a small number of European countries still outside the NATO web. These countries are under severe and sustained pressure to join NATO.
2. There is a continuing push by the NATO High Command to create new bases and place advanced weapons systems further and further to the East and right on the borders of Russia.
3. Within many of the existing NATO states in Europe there are concentrations of large military bases which, as well as being a threat to peace, are posing great environmental, economic and social problems for the host countries.

We must intensify and coordinate our efforts on all three fronts.

It was noted that April 4th 2019 is the 70th anniversary of the foundation of NATO and that we must all build in a coordinated way for a major mobilisation on that day. In light of the situation on the ground, this mobilisation will probably be three-fold: nationally, regionally at NATO Head

Office in Brussels; and also in Washington DC, USA.

There was a consensus that we need to broaden the appeal and reach of our movement and this campaign. We need to appeal to youth and students; to trade unionists; to women; to pensioners. To do this we must both ensure that our message is relevant to the lives of these sections of society and that we bring our message directly to the people to whom we wish to appeal. We may need to diversify into more modern media; to create a presence in, for example, third level colleges; to use major public events like, for example, the World Social Forum planned for Barcelona.

Because women, as the victims of war, suffer not only the threat of injury or death from direct attacks, but also suffer the danger of systemic sexual violence, including organised rape, we should make a specific appeal to women to become the promoters of peace and activists against US/NATO military bases.

We must link the criminal waste of resources and the drain on national finances through the creation of bases, the proliferation of weapons of mass destruction that are ever-more expensive, and the waging of perpetual war with the issues confronted by the people in their own lives such as a reduction in pension and other social protection payments, the lack of investment in schools and hospitals, the increased militarisation of the state and its impact on daily life.

We must also link the issue of militarisation, of which international bases are an integral part, to big ticket items like global warming; the global destruction of habitats; and the pillage of resources internationally to feed the international war machine that is NATO.

In our propaganda we must counteract the glorification of war through state-sponsored commemoration/remembrance ceremonies.

We should target the banks that are funding the military machine, specifically those funding the nuclear arms industry.

We must reclaim the United Nations as an instrument of international peace and not another arm of US/NATO imperialism.

We must directly link the issue of refugees, especially refugees attempting to enter Europe, to the open US/NATO aggression against Afghanistan, Iraq, Yemen, Syria and Libya as well as the covert activity in both North Africa and Sub-Saharan Africa.

Thank you.

Conference Closing Remarks

Bahman Azad
Coalition Against US Foreign Military Bases
USA

Thank you all. Those were great reports and we will take note of the highlights of everybody's report as much as we can. We will incorporate them and use them as a guide.

I should emphasize the two important tasks that we have set four our-selvesr in our Unity Statement: (1) "educate" and (2) "mobilise." That is an important part of our work and should be from now on. Many people don't know anything about these bases. It is important that we start an active process of educating the public about the dangers of these bases, the role of these bases and whose interests they serve.

So it is very important that we do that and in that light I wanted to mention a couple of things:

There was a suggestion that we have should have sections on the regions on our web site. We will use the web site that we created, of course — the focus of it has been basically this Conference and organising this Conference — but we want now to turn it into an information clearinghouse on US and NATO military bases. If you look at the website you will see that there are five or six tabs on the menu, with each region listed, and we have tried to include one or two or three articles in each section so as not to have it empty. But I am asking you from now on, in relation to any activity, any action, any analysis, about the bases in your region please send it to us. You have the information about the global campaign. We will try to incorporate it into the website so that people can use it as a point of reference for our struggle. That is one point.

Secondly, in light of the same objective I would like to inform you that PANA and our Coalition have agreed to collate all the presentations at this conference and publish them as "Proceedings of the First Conference." So I am asking every one of the speakers, please make sure that you have a coherent article, that you turn it into a good article — your presentation — and send it to us so that we can compile them and publish the proceedings. That is the second point.

There are a number of organisations and groups that I need to thank but I will leave that to the end. My task at this moment is to present to you for approval the draft of the Press Communiqué that was adopted by the Organising Committee of the Conference. I am going to read that now.

* * *

Press Communiqué of the First International Conference Against US/NATO Foreign Military Bases

The first International Conference against US/NATO Military Bases was held on November 16-18, at Liberty Hall in Dublin, Ireland. The Conference was attended by close to 300 participants from over thirty-five countries from around the world. Speakers representing countries from all continents, including Cuba, Argentina, Brazil, Colombia, United States, Italy, Germany, Portugal, Greece, Cyprus, Turkey, Poland, United Kingdom, Ireland, Czech Republic, Israel, Palestine, Kenya, D. R. Congo, Japan and Australia, made presentations at the conference.

This conference was the first organized effort by the newly formed Global Campaign Against US/NATO Military Bases, created by over thirty-five peace, justice and environmental organizations and endorsed by over 700 other organizations and activists from around the world. What brought all of us together in this International Conference was our agreement with the principles outlined in the Global Campaign's Unity Statement, which was endorsed by the Conference participants.

The participants in the Conference heard from and shared with representatives of organizations and movements struggling for the abolition of foreign military bases around the world about the aggression, interventions, death, destruction, and the health and environmental damage that the military bases have been causing for the whole of humanity along with the threats and violation to the sovereignty of the "host" countries.

The participants and organizers of the Conference agreed as a matter of principle that while they oppose all foreign military bases, they consider the close to 1,000 US/NATO military bases established throughout the world, which constitute the main pillars of global imperialist domination by US, NATO and EU states, as the main threat to peace and humanity, and must all be closed. The NATO states' military bases are the military expression of imperialist intervention in the lives of sovereign countries on behalf of the dominant, financial, political, and military interests, for the control of energy resources, transport roads, markets and spheres of influence, in clear violation of international law and the United Nations Charter.

The participants in the Conference call upon the organizations and movements who agree on the above to work closely with each other in a coordinated manner as a part of the Global Campaign to organize and mobilize the public around the world against US/NATO military bases.

While we call for the closure of all US/NATO military bases, we consider the closure of bases and military installations in certain countries and areas as needing special attention by the international movement. These include, for example, the Guantánamo US base in Cuba, the US bases in Okinawa and South Korea, the US Base in Rammstein/Germany, Serbia, the old and new US/NATO bases in Greece and Cyprus, the establishment of the new US African Command (AFRICOM) with its affiliated military bases in Africa, the numerous NATO bases in Italy and Scandinavia, Shannon Airport in Ireland, which is being used as a military base by US and NATO, and the newly established bases by the United States, France and their allies in and around the Syrian soil.

In order to continue our joint Global Campaign in solidarity with the just causes of the peoples in their struggle against foreign military aggression, occupation and interference in their internal affairs, and the devastating environmental and health impacts of these bases, the participants agreed to recommend and to support coordinated actions and initiatives in the coming year (2019) which shall strengthen the global movement to expand the actions and cooperation while moving forward.

As a step toward this goal, the Conference supports the global mass mobilizations against NATO's 70th anniversary Summit in Washington DC, on April 4, 2019, and respective protests in the NATO member states and worldwide.

We declare our solidarity with the Cuban people's decades-long efforts to take back their Guantánamo territory, illegally occupied by the United States, and declare our support for the Sixth International Seminar for Peace and the Abolition of Foreign Military Bases, organized by MOVPAZ for May 4-6, 2019, in Guantánamo, Cuba.

The participants express their most sincere thanks and gratitude to the Peace and Neutrality Alliance (PANA) Ireland, for their generous hospitality and support in hosting this historic Conference.

> ***Adopted by the participants at the***
> ***First International Conference***
> ***Against US/NATO Military Bases***
> ***November 18, 2018 — Dublin, Ireland***

* * *

Thank you very much everybody. It was a great victory, not only for the Conference but for the resolution.

We did it, people. We made the apparently impossible possible. And I hope this will be the beginning of very close work from now on between us; coordinating and eliminating all fragmentations that existed between us and moving forward.

A few thanks are really due, first, to PANA, as was mentioned before.

I would like to thank the staff of the Service, Industrial, Professional and Technical Union (SIPTU), not only for providing us with this great hall, but also for all the services and help we could use. I specially want to thank Brian up there, who has been sitting in the clouds, watching over us in every detail, helping and sometimes getting annoyed by me because I kept coming up with new demands and requests. He was, of course, frustrated but went out of his way to make everything possible. So I really want to thank Brian.

I would like to thank our video crew for live streaming the Conference. They had to work with me continuously from three, four days before the Conference *via* email to get rid of the glitches that we had in the system and to overcome the YouTube limiations. They were excellent, perfect and very helpful. I thank you.

And finally I want to thank our fantastic interpretation group. I am sure those of you who have been in conferences know what a difficult task it is. And they endured it today, yesterday and the day before yesterday. I thank both of you.

So, let me call upon my partner in crime, Roger Cole, to make some Conference closing remarks.

Conference Closing Remarks

Roger Cole
Peace and Neutrality Alliance
Ireland

Thank you all for attending the First International Conference Against US/NATO Military Bases in Liberty Hall, Dublin.

I hope you all thought it was worthwhile, learnt more, made friends, and got some time to see Dublin.

Humanity is facing two major threats, global war and global warming, and the two are linked, as global warming will mean more wars over resources. The immediate threat of global war, however, has increased with the decision of the US to withdraw from the Intermediate Nuclear Weapons (INF) Treaty, which is why our global campaign is a crucial step towards peace. While several countries have foreign military bases, the reality is the US has far more foreign military bases than all other countries, is committed to the doctrine of perpetual war and by withdrawing from the INF Treaty has greatly increased the chance of global nuclear war.

The Conference covered a very wide number of issues, which have been recorded, so there is no need to mention them all.

However, I will say it was a very successful conference, and the core reason for that success was the Unity Statement.

In the weeks and months ahead we need to focus on getting more and more peace groups to sign up to the unity statement. We need to ensure that if we are to avoid global war we have to build a united global peace movement.

The Unity Statement is the key document in achieving that unity. Let there be no doubt that the advocates of global war are united.

The imperial nature of the US/EU/NATO axis is its unity, and while there are differences within the axis, all the evidence shows that their unity and support for war is much greater than their differences.

If we are to defeat them, then we must be united. Even if we are united, it will not be easy, but there is one reality: if we are not united, they will win.

The core of this Conference is opposition to imperial wars, and opposition to imperialism is the core reason for the establishment of PANA in 1996. Anti-imperialism is in our DNA, a DNA that is deeply rooted in the hearts and minds of the Irish people, and the reason for that is the consequence of our history.

To give a few examples: when Oliver Cromwell and his army conquered Ireland between 1649 and 1652, a third of the Irish people were killed; in the great famine in the 19th Century, under the rule of his British imperial successors, one million Irish people died and one million were forced to emigrate. So no wonder anti-imperialism is so deeply rooted among us.

PANA knows, however, that opposition to imperialist wars is not uniquely Irish, which is why we supported this Global Conference.

However, even in Ireland, there have always been those that supported imperialism, especially the rich and powerful, and they have not gone away you know. Over three million US troops and an unknown amount of US military equipment have landed at Shannon Airport on their way to the perpetual wars of the US.

They support the abolition of the Irish Army and its integration into a "true" European Army as advocated by Macron and Merkel.

This support for imperialist wars has been made crystal clear by the refusal of the Irish corporate media, which is owned and controlled by the ruling Irish class, to give this Global Conference (with the exception of the Belfast Newsletter) any coverage whatsoever, just like they give little or no coverage to the US' use of Shannon Airport.

However, the recently democratically re-elected President of Ireland, Michael D. Higgins, by raising the issue of Permanent Structural Cooperation (PESCO), which is the mechanism by which the EU Army is being created, during the election campaign, by inviting me, as Chair of PANA to his inauguration ceremony in Dublin Castle, and, more importantly, by inviting one of our main speakers, Aida Touma Sliman, to Áras an Uachtaráin, [the President's residence], the President, who was re-elected in a landslide with 822,566 first preference votes, was indicating his opposition to the media blackout of this conference and the anti-imperialist struggle that is at the core of our message.

Finally while Bahman has thanked everybody, he left out one person — himself. Without his organization ability, skill and commitment, there would have been no conference.

Let us commit ourselves to building a global peace movement, by ensuring more groups and people endorse the Unity Statement, so that our next Global Conference is stronger and more powerful than ever.